CHRISTIANITY
E✝PLORED

Authentic
LIFESTYLE

First published in 2001 by Paternoster Lifestyle
Second edition published in 2003 by Authentic Lifestyle
Reprinted 2003 (twice)

09 08 07 06 05 04 03   9 8 7 6 5 4 3

Authentic Lifestyle is an imprint of Authentic Media,
PO Box 300, Carlisle, Cumbria, CA3 0QS, UK
And PO Box 1047, Waynesboro, GA 30830-2047, USA
www.paternoster-publishing.com

British Library Cataloguing in Publication Data
A catalogue record for this book is available from the British Library

ISBN 1-85078-522-8

Unless otherwise stated, Scripture quotations are taken from the
HOLY BIBLE, NEW INTERNATIONAL VERSION
Copyright © 1973, 1978, 1984 by the International Bible Society.
Used by permission of Hodder and Stoughton Limited. All rights reserved.
'NIV' is a registered trademark of the International Bible Society
UK trademark number 1448790

Designed by Diane Bainbridge
Printed in Great Britain by Bell and Bain, Glasgow

CHRISTIANITY EXPLORED

HOW TO RUN

THE COURSE

"If life had a second edition, how I would correct the proofs."

John Clare

Christianity Explored is a ten-week course that aims to introduce people to Jesus Christ.

As Mark's Gospel is read, taught and discussed, participants explore three questions that cut right to the heart of Christianity: Who was Jesus? Why did he come? And what does Jesus demand of those who want to follow him?

This second edition of *Christianity Explored* incorporates much of the feedback that has been received since it was first published. In particular, the course structure is now much easier to follow, Bible studies have been revised and the training material has been refined.

As ever, feel free to adapt the material to suit you and your situation, but – as the course is the result of many years of experience – it is a good idea to use *Christianity Explored* "as is" at least once before making significant changes to it. And if you do decide to run *Christianity Explored*, please let us know when and where your course is running. Visit www.christianityexplored.com, or write to the Project Manager, Christianity Explored, All Souls Church, Langham Place, London, W1B 3DA, United Kingdom.

What makes the Christian gospel distinctive is its insistence on God's remarkable grace: the clear teaching that although we human beings are rotten to the core, we are loved. Loved with an outrageous, daring, incomprehensible love, and what's more, loved by the very being whose love we have treated as if it were unworthy of us.

As a result, *Christianity Explored* should be a disturbing experience for everyone. It should be no easier for leaders to relate Jesus' teaching on sin, judgement, wrath and hell than it is for a course participant to hear it. But, if we are prepared to trust in the Holy Spirit's power to open blind eyes, these uncomfortable truths pave the way for a faithful life lived in gratitude for God's unmerited love.

USING THE RESOURCES

All of these resources are available in Christian book stores or from www.christianityexplored.com

The **STUDY GUIDE** is intended for each course participant and includes a brief introduction to the course, outlines of the talks and studies to work through week by week.

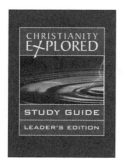

The **STUDY GUIDE - LEADER'S EDITION** is intended for leaders and contains all the above material, as well as answers to the studies and additional notes to help leaders prepare for each week on the course. There is also a section to help leaders teach Mark's Gospel and evangelize faithfully.

CHRISTIANITY
EXPLORED

The **VIDEOS** are intended for course leaders who are unable to prepare and deliver talks each week. Filmed on location around the UK, the fourteen talks feature on-screen Bible text. Also included is a short booklet explaining how to use the videos as part of a *Christianity Explored* course.

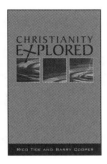

CHRISTIANITY EXPLORED is a stand-alone paperback book based on the course. A jargon-free introduction to Jesus Christ, it can be used as a means of encouraging people to join a course, to help participants consolidate what they have learned, or to reach those who would rather not attend a course.

The **WEBSITE** is a further resource for leaders and participants. You can find it at www.christianityexplored.com

SETTING UP THE COURSE

The *Christianity Explored* course consists of Bible studies, talks or videos, and group discussions. You, as course leader, are responsible for "hosting" the evening. In other words, you will do everything that requires "leading from the front."

STRUCTURE OF THE COURSE

	GROUP DISCUSSION 1	TALK / VIDEO	GROUP DISCUSSION 2	HOME STUDY
WEEK 1	Welcome	Introduction	Discuss Talk / Video	Mark 1:1 – 3:6
WEEK 2	Mark 2:1–12	Jesus – Who Was He?	Discuss Talk / Video	Mark 3:7 – 5:43
WEEK 3	Mark 4:35–41	Jesus – Why Did He Come?	Discuss Talk / Video	Mark 6:1 – 8:29
WEEK 4	Mark 8:17–29	Jesus – His Death	Discuss Talk / Video	Mark 8:30 – 10:52
WEEK 5	Mark 10:17–22	What is Grace?	Discuss Talk / Video	Mark 11:1 – 13:37
WEEK 6	Mark 12:1–11	Jesus – His Resurrection	Discuss Talk / Video	Mark 14:1 – 16:8
EXPLORING CHRISTIAN LIFE		The Church	Discuss Talk / Video	
		The Holy Spirit	Discuss Talk / Video	
		Prayer	Discuss Talk / Video	
		The Bible	Discuss Talk / Video	
WEEK 7	Mark 14:1–11	What is a Christian?	Discuss Talk / Video	Ephesians 2:1–22
WEEK 8	Ephesians 2:1–10	Continuing as a Christian	Discuss Talk / Video	Mark 3:1 – 4:41
WEEK 9	Mark 4:3–20	Choices – King Herod	Discuss Talk / Video	Any questions?
WEEK 10	Any questions?	Choices – James, John & Bartimaeus	Discuss Talk / Video	

The first six weeks focus on who Jesus is and why he came. In particular, course participants explore the problem of sin and the wonder of forgiveness. Then, during a weekend or day away, participants discover the importance of the church, the Holy Spirit, prayer and the Bible. The objective in the final weeks is to emphasize Christ's call in Mark 8:34: "If anyone would come after me, he must deny himself and take up his cross and follow me."

STRUCTURE OF THE EVENING

Below is the suggested structure for the evening. See Session 5 of the training notes in the *Study Guide – Leader's Edition* for a fuller description of each component. Of course, depending on your circumstances, you might want to change the exact times. Equally, you might want to run the course during the day if that is a more suitable time for those you're trying to reach.

6:30 p.m.	**Leaders' prayer meeting**
7:00 p.m.	**Participants arrive for the meal**
7:45 p.m.	**GROUP DISCUSSION 1**
8:05 p.m.	**Talk / Video**
8:30 p.m.	**GROUP DISCUSSION 2**
9:00 p.m.	**End of the evening – "One-to-One"**

Note: All times are approximate. You can make certain sessions shorter or longer depending on your circumstances.

You can run **Christianity Explored** with videos or with talks presented by the course leader.

If you decide to run the course with the videos, see the *Guide to Using the Videos* (included with the video cassettes). Please note that because the videos feature on-screen Bible text, it is inadvisable to use them with large groups unless you have access to a projection screen and projector.

If you decide to run the course with the talks, see the section entitled "The Talks" in this book. Delivering the talks yourself will lead to a more personal, more intimate experience for the participants.

It is important to make participants feel relaxed and welcome, and the way you set up your venue will help you achieve that.

If there are a large number of leaders and participants, set up a number of tables around which different groups can sit. Because each group will be engaged in separate discussions, remember to leave plenty of space between tables so that participants and leaders can hear each other easily.

- You will need a way of displaying visual aids (PowerPoint, overhead projector or flipchart).

- Ensure that everyone can see. TVs, screens and any visual aids (not to mention the person giving the talk) should be visible from anywhere in the room.

- Make sure that facilities and exits are clearly marked.

- You may like to set aside a table with a selection of books for participants and leaders to buy or borrow.[1]

Everyone involved in the course – leaders, participants and the course leader – will need a Bible. It is important that everyone use the same version and edition so that page numbers will be the same. (The version used throughout the course material is the New International Version.)

- Participants should each be given a Bible at the beginning of the course, preferably one they can keep when the course ends.

- They should also be given a copy of the *Study Guide*.

- Pens should be made available to allow participants to make notes or jot down questions.

---

[1] The **Christianity Explored** website lists a number of recommended books on various subjects. Visit the "Running a Course" section at www.christianityexplored.com

The hardest part of **Christianity Explored** for many participants is getting through the door on the first night. This will be especially true if you're running your course in a church building, which for many will seem an unfamiliar, unwelcoming place.

A team of "welcomers" should be given the task of greeting participants as they arrive. Choose welcomers who are not leaders: that way, leaders can concentrate on talking to participants who've already arrived.

When a participant arrives, welcomers should simply introduce themselves and find out the person's name. Asking for addresses or telephone numbers at this stage can make people feel uncomfortable.

If you're expecting a large number of participants, it's a good idea to prepare a seating plan like the one below.

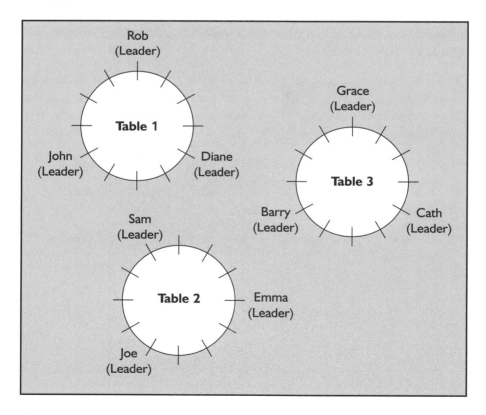

Then, as each participant arrives, a welcomer assigns him or her to a table and adds the person's name to the plan. This ensures that participants are divided equally between the tables.

Numbering the tables "restaurant-style" will help participants to find their allocated table easily.

Leaders and welcomers should wear name tags so that they are immediately identifiable by participants.

➤ *Write down the names of people you will ask to join "The Welcome Team."*

THE CATERING TEAM

Sharing a meal together is a core component of **Christianity Explored**. It's an opportunity to socialize informally and, for many participants, it will be the only time during the week when someone takes a genuine, personal interest in their lives.

Organize a team of people who are willing and able to prepare and serve a meal. If necessary, you can ask participants for a small contribution to help defray the cost.

➤ *Write down the names of people you will ask to join "The Catering Team."*

Enlisting people to pray regularly for the course is a wonderful way of involving more people in **Christianity Explored**. Report back to your prayer team on a weekly basis so that they can pray for specific needs and be encouraged by answered prayer.

➤ *Write down the names of people you will ask to join "The Prayer Team."*

CHOOSING AND TRAINING LEADERS

As course leader, you will need to choose and train leaders who will be responsible for those who attend the course.

CHOOSING LEADERS

Leaders should be mature Christians who are able to teach, encourage discussion and care for participants.

In selecting a leader, ask yourself, "Is this person able to teach the Bible faithfully and clearly? Will he or she be able to deal with difficult questions on Mark's Gospel?"

Secondly, ask yourself, "Will this person be able to promote discussion without dominating it?" Since so much of the course revolves around discussion, participants should feel free to be open and honest in their group.

Thirdly, ask yourself, "Is this the type of person who would make a participant feel welcome and cared for?" Rather than simply telling people about God's love, leaders must be willing to demonstrate that love by devoting time and attention to those in their care.

And of course, a leader's responsibility goes beyond ten weeks. Relationships begun during the course are likely to develop into friendships that must be nurtured once the course is over. For this reason, it is inadvisable to ask leaders to take on more than one course a year.

- A high ratio of leaders to participants is essential. A well-balanced group will typically consist of three leaders and nine participants.

- In order to deal with pastoral situations appropriately, it's advisable to assign a mixture of male and female leaders to each team.

- Make a list of all your leaders and then divide them into teams of three.

➤ *Write down a list of your leaders and divide them into teams of three.*

TRAINING LEADERS

A training day should take place before the course begins. Once a leader understands the reasoning behind the course, it becomes much easier for him or her to commit the time required. As well as preparing leaders for the course, the training day cements relationships between those who will be leading together.

You should therefore have a training day before every course you run, and all leaders should be asked to attend – even if they have been leaders many times before. Feel free to vary the exercises so the training remains fresh for veteran leaders.

• Ensure that every leader (including yourself) has a copy of the *Study Guide – Leader's Edition*, which contains the nine training sessions.

• You, as the course leader, should lead the nine sessions.

• The sessions should be read aloud, allowing time for the teams of leaders to complete the exercises involved.

	Pray	
SESSION 1	**Why Evangelize?**	30 minutes
SESSION 2	**God's Part in Evangelism – and Ours**	30 minutes
SESSION 3	**Being a Christianity Explored Leader**	15 minutes
SESSION 4	**Before the Course**	25 minutes
	Pray	
	Lunch	
SESSION 5	**During the Course**	45 minutes
SESSION 6	**Explore, Explain, Encourage**	60 minutes
	Coffee	
SESSION 7	**Identity, Mission, Call**	90 minutes
	Coffee	
SESSION 8	**After the Course**	15 minutes
SESSION 9	**Getting our Expectations Right**	20 minutes
	Pray	

INVITING PARTICIPANTS

Although some people will immediately respond positively to an invitation to attend *Christianity Explored*, others will be more reluctant. It's more than likely that they'll be thinking one of three thoughts:

- Christians are weird
  I don't have anything in common with them.

- Christianity is irrelevant
  It's of no practical use to my life.

- Christianity is untrue
  Why should there be only one way to heaven, and why should it have anything to do with Jesus?

Overcoming these objections is a gradual process, and it may be years before some people agree to join a course. Inviting people to events is a great way of helping them to overcome their objections.

VENUE-BASED EVENTS

These events are for people who think that Christians are weird. People who think like this are unlikely to come anywhere near a church.

Venue-based events get around this by enabling people to meet credible Christians outside the church environment.

Think of events you could run in your local area that would appeal to non-Christians (dance lessons, a trip to a place with historic significance, a football game, a visit to an art gallery, a barbecue, etc.).

At such an event, there should be a short Christian talk or testimony, and an invitation to come to *Christianity Explored* to find out more – not an invitation to make a commitment to Jesus Christ.

TOPIC-BASED EVENTS

These events are for people who think that Christianity is irrelevant. People who think like this are unaware that the Bible is God speaking today.

Topic-based events get around this by enabling people to hear talks that address contemporary issues from a Christian perspective.

Think of speakers you could ask to present talks on issues that are important to those you're trying to reach (parenting, stress, genetics, fashion, ambition, etc.).

Again, at such an event, there should be an invitation to come to **Christianity Explored** to find out more.

CHURCH-BASED EVENTS

These events are for people who think that Christianity is untrue. People who think like this are unlikely to have heard the gospel preached in years, if at all.

Church-based events get around this by enabling people to attend a church service where the gospel is clearly presented.

Think of ways in which you could specifically tailor a service for such a person (choose hymns with familiar melodies, avoid using Christian "jargon" without carefully explaining it first, make sure the church is warm and welcoming, include testimonies from people who have attended the course, etc.).

Again, at such an event, there should be an invitation to come to **Christianity Explored** to find out more.

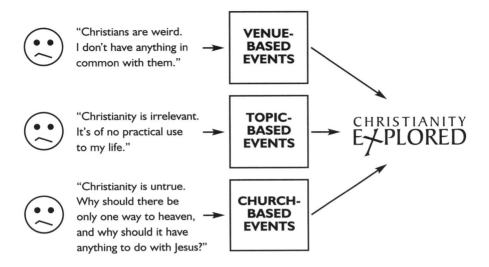

- Schedule your events to take place about two weeks before the course begins. Make sure that your church members know about the events in advance, are praying for them, and inviting people to them.

- Get your church involved in planning events. What are your church members passionate about? Could they base an event around that subject?

- Make sure your church members understand the content and reasoning behind the course so that they'll have confidence to invite their friends to events.

- When inviting people to events or to *Christianity Explored*, it is important to be honest about exactly what will happen and who will be there.

- Make "contact cards" and pens available during events so that people can write down their contact details if they're interested in coming to a course. Phone them the week before and remind them that the course is about to begin.

- If an event doesn't go well, celebrate the fact that people have tried.

You might want to leave invitations such as the one below at the entrance of your church. It's also a good idea to make them freely available for church members to use when inviting friends, family or colleagues.

CHRISTIANITY
E✝PLORED

You don't need to know anything about the Bible.

You won't be asked to read aloud, pray or sing.

You can ask any question you want.

DAY Wednesday evenings

TIME 7 p.m. to 9 p.m.

VENUE Church, Street, City

DATES From 9th October to 11th December

If you'd like to come or want to find out more, please contact ....

Another way of inviting people is to use a survey like the one on the next page. You could make the surveys available at a church service, or even try the survey on people in the street, telling them: "We're from .... Church, and we're doing a survey of people's beliefs – would you have five minutes to answer a few questions?"

1. What do you think is the purpose of life?

- [ ] There is no purpose
- [ ] Sexual fulfillment
- [ ] Love
- [ ] Achieving personal spiritual goals
- [ ] Saving the environment
- [ ] Worshipping and serving a god
- [ ] Achieving personal goals
- [ ] Having a good time
- [ ] Making money
- [ ] Achieving social political goals
- [ ] Job satisfaction
- [ ] Serving other people
- [ ] Advancement of humanity
- [ ] Friendship
- [ ] Don't know

2. How important is the spiritual dimension in your life?

- [ ] Very
- [ ] Fairly
- [ ] Unimportant
- [ ] There isn't one
- [ ] Don't know

3. What do you think happens when a person dies?

- [ ] Heaven or hell
- [ ] Reincarnation
- [ ] Heaven for everyone
- [ ] Nothing
- [ ] Purgatory
- [ ] Don't know
- [ ] Another spiritual plane
- [ ] Other

4. What is your view of the Bible?

- [ ] No longer relevant
- [ ] Unreliable document of historical interest
- [ ] Important religious text
- [ ] Myth / Fable
- [ ] God's message to people
- [ ] Don't know
- [ ] Moral code
- [ ] A good story
- [ ] Other

5. What led you to this conclusion?

- [ ] Family
- [ ] Media
- [ ] Don't know
- [ ] Spiritual experience
- [ ] Own investigation
- [ ] Other
- [ ] Education
- [ ] Experience of life
- [ ] Religious texts
- [ ] Friends

6. What is your view of Christ?

- [ ] Didn't exist
- [ ] Deluded
- [ ] Prophet
- [ ] Good man
- [ ] Deceiver
- [ ] Don't know
- [ ] Moral teacher
- [ ] Political figure
- [ ] Other
- [ ] God in human form
- [ ] Mythical figure

7. What led you to this conclusion?

- [ ] Family
- [ ] Experience of life
- [ ] Don't know
- [ ] Spiritual experience
- [ ] Friends
- [ ] Other
- [ ] Education
- [ ] Religious texts
- [ ] Own investigation
- [ ] Media

8. If you could ask God one question, and you knew it would answered, what would it be?

Thank you for taking time to complete this questionnaire.

We're also giving out leaflets containing a short explanation of the Christian faith. Would you like to take one?

- [ ] Yes
- [ ] No

We run a course called *Christianity Explored*. You can ask any question you want in a relaxed environment – you won't be asked to pray, sing, read or anything like that, and you won't be pestered if you decide not to come again.

Would you be interested in trying such a course?
- [ ] Yes
- [ ] No

If yes, please write your name and a contact number / e-mail below:

➤ *Write down your ideas for events you might run.*

ORGANIZING THE WEEKEND OR DAY AWAY

People need to have a clear understanding of what the Christian life entails before committing to it. With that in mind, the "Exploring Christian Life" weekend or day away has been placed before Weeks 7–10, when participants are invited to repent and believe.

The material covered during this time aims to paint a realistic picture of what the Christian life is like, and to reassure people that they will not be alone if they choose to begin following Christ. Participants are given the chance to count the cost and are assured that God will graciously provide the church family, his Holy Spirit, prayer and the Bible to uphold them.

- In Week 4, let participants know that there will be a weekend or day away. Give a brief idea of what will happen, and ask them to block out the time in their diaries. (If your participants lead particularly busy lives you may need to do this sooner.)

- In Weeks 5 and 6, hand out invitations and schedules for the weekend or day. (Most participants like to have information about what is planned before they decide to come.)

- Leaders will need to encourage participants to sign up for the weekend or day away.

- It is important for leaders to attend if participants in their care have signed up.

- Ensure that your prayer team has been notified and that they are praying ahead.

- During the weekend or day away, there should be no singing, praying or anything that could make participants feel unduly pressured or uncomfortable.

- The weekend or day away allows plenty of time for leaders to continue to build trusting relationships with participants. Use the free time for activities that will facilitate this (for example, walks in the country, playing a team sport or visiting local attractions).

- Leaders' testimonies are also important, because they give participants an insight into the practicalities of Christian living. Choose leaders to present their testimonies and help them to prepare what they will say. (Practical advice on preparing testimonies can also be found in Session 4 of the training notes in the *Study Guide – Leader's Edition*). Testimonies can be presented at any point during the weekend or day away.

CHRISTIANITY
E✝PLORED

16th – 18th June

Feel like escaping for the weekend? Why not join us for a relaxing time in the country. Enjoy good company and excellent teaching in the comfort of Woodcote Lodge, Sunnydale.

The weekend will provide an ideal opportunity to get to know one another better, and to think through what the Bible says about being a Christian. You can participate as much or as little as you like.

It's reasonably priced at £30 per person, which includes a non-returnable deposit of £10. Some subsidies are also available and can be discussed with the leaders.

Please complete the slip below and give it to your leader if you'd like to come. We'll be leaving the church at 7 p.m. on the 16th.

....

NAME: _____

TELEPHONE: _____

ADDRESS: _____

_____

Who are your **Christianity Explored** leaders? _____

Any special dietary requirements? _____

I enclose a cheque for £ _____ made payable to Hilltop Church.

I can/cannot offer transport to _____ people.

I require transport ☐ Yes   ☐ No

FRIDAY

    Arrive   9:00 p.m.

    Welcome   9:30 p.m.

SATURDAY

    Leaders' prayer meeting   8:30 a.m.

    Breakfast   9:00 a.m.

    Exploring Christian Life – The Church   10:00 a.m.
    followed by group discussion

    Coffee   11:30 a.m.

    Exploring Christian Life – The Holy Spirit   12:00 p.m.
    followed by group discussion

    Lunch   1:30 p.m.

    Free afternoon   2:30 p.m.

    Dinner   6:30 p.m.

    Exploring Christian Life – Prayer   7:30 p.m.
    followed by group discussion

    Free evening   9:00 p.m.

SUNDAY

    Leaders' prayer meeting   9:30 a.m.

    Breakfast   10:00 a.m.

    Exploring Christian Life – The Bible   11:00 a.m.
    followed by group discussion

    Lunch   12:30 p.m.

    Leave   1:30 p.m.

CHRISTIANITY
EXPLORED

17th June

Feel like escaping for the day? Why not join us for a relaxing day of food, conversation and a few more short videos? It'll be a chance to enjoy some good company and teaching in an unhurried atmosphere. Lunch (and popcorn!) will be provided.

Time: **10 a.m. until 7 p.m.**

Place: **Woodcote Lodge, Sunnydale**

Just complete the slip below if you would like to come, then give it to your leader.

....

NAME: _____

TELEPHONE: _____

ADDRESS: _____

_____

Who are your *Christianity Explored* leaders? _____

Any special dietary requirements? _____

I can/cannot offer transport to _____ people.

I require transport ☐ Yes ☐ No

Arrive	10:00 a.m.
Welcome and coffee	10:30 a.m.
Exploring Christian Life – The Church followed by group discussion	11:00 a.m.
Coffee	12:00 p.m.
Exploring Christian Life – The Holy Spirit followed by group discussion	12:30 p.m.
Lunch	1:30 p.m.
Free time	2:30 p.m.
Exploring Christian Life – Prayer followed by group discussion	4:30 p.m.
Coffee	5:30 p.m.
Exploring Christian Life – The Bible followed by group discussion	6:00 p.m.
Leave	7:00 p.m.

CHRISTIANITY
EXPLORED

GETTING FEEDBACK

As a course leader, it's very helpful to find out what you're doing right, and perhaps ways in which you might improve future courses. Give out feedback forms to leaders and participants at the end of Week 10. Not only will they be helpful to you, but they will also help everyone involved with the course to reflect on their own progress.

EXAMPLE FEEDBACK FORM FOR LEADERS

We are always seeking to improve *Christianity Explored* and would value your feedback. The training of leaders is an essential part of the course and your comments would be very much appreciated. Please be as honest as possible.

1 **What did you find most enriching about leading?**

2 **What did you find most difficult about leading?**

3 **How did you find the leaders' training prior to the course?**

4 **Could we have prepared you better for the course? If so, how?**

5 **How did you find the leaders' prayer meetings?**

6 **What did you think of the course material?**

7 **Do you have any comments to make on the weekend or day away? How could it be improved?**

8 **Please feel free to comment on any other aspects of the course.**

You don't have to answer all the questions if you don't want to, but please be as honest as you can.

Your details (optional):

Name _____ Date _____

Address _____

Telephone _____ E-mail _____

1 Before you began *Christianity Explored*, how would you have described yourself?

☐ I didn't believe in God

☐ I wasn't sure if God existed or not

☐ I believed in God but not in Jesus Christ

☐ A Christian (that is, personally committed to Jesus Christ)

☐ Something else _____

2 How would you assess your position now in relation to Jesus Christ?

☐ I understand who Jesus is, why he came and what it means to follow him.
I have put my trust in him.

☐ I am interested in learning more but, as yet, I have not put my trust in Jesus

☐ Other _____

3 If you have not yet put your trust in Jesus, what is stopping you?

4 Do you know for certain that you have eternal life?

☐ Yes   ☐ No

5 Suppose you were to die tonight and God asked, "Why should I let you into heaven?" What would you say?

6 What would you like to do now?

☐ I am interested in joining a follow-up course (a course that will help me to continue in the Christian life).

☐ I would like to come to *Christianity Explored* again.

☐ I would like a copy of the *Christianity Explored* book in order to review what I've learned.

☐ I do not wish to do anything further at this stage.

☐ I would like to join a church.

☐ I am happy at the church I go to, which is _____

7 Would you like to make any comments about the course, either positive or negative?

CHRISTIANITY
EXPLORED

➤ Once you have run a **Christianity Explored** course, use this space to write down the things that went well and the things you might do differently next time.

CHRISTIANITY EXPLORED

THE TALKS

The talks included in this section are transcripts of the material presented by Rico Tice at All Souls Church in London.

Most of the personal illustrations used by Rico have been cut from these transcripts, but some have been preserved to demonstrate the importance of genuine, real-life testimony during the talks. For your reference, Rico's personal illustrations have been italicized and indented. Of course, you will want to insert illustrations from your own experience and adapt the style to make the talks work as effectively as possible. This is especially true in Weeks 3, 4 and 6, when warmth and humanity are essential in order to win a hearing for the biblical truths contained within.

The visual aids needed are placed in boxes. These should be made into a PowerPoint presentation or into transparencies and displayed using an overhead projector. If you don't have access to PowerPoint or an overhead projector, you can write out the visual aids on a flipchart and have them ready to display each week. Downloadable versions of the visual aids are available from the "Running a Course" section on the website at www.christianityexplored.com

Don't forget to let us know if you decide to run *Christianity Explored*. Tell us when and where your course is running by visiting the website, or by writing to: Project Manager, Christianity Explored, All Souls Church, Langham Place, London, W1B 3DA, United Kingdom.

INTRODUCTION

BEFORE THE TALK

➤ *Welcome the course participants and take 5 minutes to work through the* Study Guide *section called GROUP DISCUSSION 1.*

➤ *Give a brief introduction. The wording below is intended only as a general guide.*

As we begin, I want to reassure you that:

• You won't be asked to read aloud, pray, sing or do anything that makes you feel uncomfortable.

• We aren't going to take your phone number and pester you. If you decide you aren't going to come back, I'm still delighted you made time to come this week.

• You can ask any question you want, or alternatively feel free just to sit and listen.

Over the next ten weeks, we'll be exploring some tough questions:

• Does God exist?

• What is the meaning of our brief lives?

• Where are we going?

• Can we know contentment and happiness?

• Why is there pain and suffering in the world?

And we want to spend time addressing whatever questions are important to you.

> ➤ *Deliver the talk. The wording below is intended only as a general guide. The aim of this talk is to confront participants' preconceptions about Christianity, show that Christianity is "good news" about Jesus Christ (Mark 1:1), and challenge them to discover what that "good news" is by making time to read Mark's Gospel.*

The world around us makes us ask questions, doesn't it?

> I remember watching the sun go down on Table Mountain in South Africa. Some cloud drifted in until we were looking down through it onto Cape Town. The memory of that sunset will stay with me till I die. It was so beautiful that for a full 15 minutes those I was with, including a little boy of eight, were speechless.

Maybe you can think of a time when you were overwhelmed by a sense of the wonder of nature. It makes us instinctively ask, "Where does it all come from?"

I wonder how you answer that question. Some people are convinced that the world sprang into being by chance, but others think that our universe – and everything in it – was deliberately created by God. Sir James Jeans, the famous British astronomer, once said: "The universe appears to have been designed by a pure Mathematician."[1] For him, as for many, the order of the earth and the solar system points to a master planner.

Take, for example, the fact that the earth is tilted at an angle of exactly 23 degrees. Scientists tell us that if the angle were even slightly different, the earth would gradually be encased by an ice cap. It has to be exactly 23 degrees to work.

Or what about the galaxy we live in? There are apparently 400 billion stars in our Milky Way galaxy alone, and there are estimated to be over 100 billion galaxies in the universe.

Now, in Psalm 8 King David wrote: "When I consider your heavens, the work of your fingers, the moon and the stars, which you have set in place, what is man[2] that you are mindful of him, the son of man that you care for him?" These verses tell us that God has set this whole universe in place and holds it as you or I might hold a contact lens on our finger.

---

[1] Sir James Jeans, *The Mysterious Universe* (Cambridge: Cambridge University Press, 1932), p. 140.
[2] You may wish to point out that the word "man" here refers to all mankind (in other words, all human beings).

How do we know that we matter to God, and that he is "mindful" of human beings? Well, this immense and awesome God is not just concerned with the stars and the planets. He also created the molecules, the neutrons, the protons. He made the 75,000 miles of blood vessels in the human body that carry blood to over 60 trillion cells. In the woodpecker he created the tiny sponge-like pad between the bill and the head so that when he drills a hole he doesn't knock himself out. That may not be important to you, but it's very important to the woodpecker!

But what's *your* picture of God? What do you think of him? What are your big questions? We want to start some discussion in your groups now and we'd like to find out three things:

➤ *Display the following questions and read them aloud.*

- **What's your name?**

- **Why are you here?**

- **If you could ask God one question, and you knew it would be answered, what would it be?**

The second question – "Why are you here?" – is not "I'm a piece of DNA stranded in the universe." It's just, "How did you happen to come along this evening?"

As for the third question, there's a great John Travolta movie where someone tells him: "If my answers frighten you, then you should cease asking scary questions."[3]

Well, we're not afraid of scary questions. Maybe you've had one on your mind a long time. So please be honest and don't hold back.

If you turn to page 12 in your *Study Guide*, there is room to write out your answer to this question.

➤ *Allow 15 minutes for groups to discuss these questions, making it clear that there will be more time for discussion later on.*

---

3 *Pulp Fiction* (dir. Quentin Tarantino; prod. Lawrence Bender; Miramax Films, 1994).

OK, thanks everyone. I don't know what your questions are: some may be very personal, others quite academic, but I do hope we make some progress with them. If they are important to you, they are important to us.

I think it's fair to say that underlying most people's questions are two issues: firstly, is there a God? And second, if there is a God, what is he, she or it like?

Now, according to opinion polls, most people believe that there is a God.[4] But the thing that really baffles them is, "If God *is* there, how can I know what he's like, and how am I supposed to relate to him?"

> *I had real difficulty with that question for a long time. When I was a child, my mother used to take us to church occasionally and I just found it so boring. If I was supposed to relate to God in some way, I couldn't see what on earth church had to do with it. I was so bored, I can remember sitting there and counting the bricks up the wall.*

It may be that you've tried to relate to God in the past by going to church, but for one reason or another you've found it boring, so you've left with the impression that Christianity as a whole is boring.

Or maybe you think that the Bible is irrelevant. After all, it was written 2,000 years ago and 2,000 miles away. What relevance could it possibly have for us?

> *I thought it was just a book of rules. In fact it seemed so irrelevant to me that I used to amuse myself in religious education classes by trying to make it relevant. I spent my time looking for references to rugby football. The one I was particularly proud of was where John chapter 9, verse 1 talks about referees: "A man blind from birth."*

Or maybe you think that Christianity is simply untrue.

> *I thought it was all a world of make-believe that belonged to the nursery, so Jesus walking on the water, the three wise men, the feeding of the five thousand, Santa Claus and Winnie the Pooh were all mixed up in my mind together.*

---

[4] *Social Trends* 30 (eds. Jil Matheson and Carol Summerfield; National Statistics, Crown Copyright 2000; London: The Stationery Office, 2000), p. 219, section 13.20.

CHRISTIANITY
E✝PLORED

But all of these preconceptions are wiped out by one verse in the Bible. Have a look at the book of Mark chapter 1, verse 1. You can find it on page ..... of your Bible.

➤ *Open your own Bible and read aloud from it.*

It says: "The beginning of the gospel about Jesus Christ, the Son of God."

So Christianity is *not* primarily about:

• going to church,
• obeying rules,
• or getting baptized.

And it's not about:

• beautiful buildings,
• or a God whose only aim in life is to stop me from having fun.

No, it's about Jesus Christ. The word "gospel" means "good news," so Mark chapter 1, verse 1 tells us that the gospel – the good news, Christianity – is all about Jesus Christ. Mark 1, verse 1 doesn't say the beginning of the gospel about keeping rules and being miserable. No, it says the beginning of the gospel about Jesus Christ.

Nor is this the beginning of the gospel about "throwing your brain out of the window." You don't have to suspend your mental faculties to believe in Jesus, because he is a real person who lived and walked and talked in human history. He is someone who can be investigated.

So back to the question: "How can I know what God is like and how am I supposed to relate to him?" One of the great things about Jesus Christ is that when we look at him, the guessing games about God stop. Because the Bible says that God has shown us what he is like by sending his Son, Jesus Christ. Colossians chapter 1, verse 15 says that Jesus is "the visible image of the invisible God."

Imagine wanting to get to know Queen Elizabeth personally:

• you could write her a letter;
• you could ring Buckingham Palace;
• or you could stand outside her gates with a big sign asking her out to lunch.

But of course you wouldn't get very far with any of these approaches. Your only chance of getting to know her would be if *she* came out to meet *you*. And that is what the Bible says God has done by sending his Son, Jesus Christ. God wants to introduce himself to us, and Jesus is the way he's chosen to do it.

I'm sure you've had the experience of walking down the main street in a busy city and being offered a leaflet which you ignore – or take and then ignore – because you don't think it'll do you any good. Well, the *Evening Standard* newspaper conducted an experiment. They got a man to stand outside Oxford Circus station offering people a leaflet. On the leaflet was the free offer of £5 for just bringing the leaflet back to the man. Hordes of people passed him, and in three hours only eleven came back for the £5. People assumed they knew what he was handing out and that it would do them no good, so they didn't bother to take it or read it.

My plea is that you don't make the same mistake with the Bible, because it's our main source of information about Jesus. If you want to find out what God is like, and how you're supposed to relate to him, then this

➤ *Hold up a Bible.*

is all you need.

However, like any relationship, this will take time. We live in an age of instant things, don't we?

- Instant credit;
- Instant coffee;
- Instant communication.

But relationships aren't instant. They take time. Please don't say, "I went one week and tried it but it didn't work." I know that, for many of you, time is a very precious commodity. But the urgent is always the enemy of the important. So do please make time to find out about these things.

➤ *For the following illustrations, use books and personalities appropriate to your context and, if possible, hold up any books you refer to.*

CHRISTIANITY
E✝PLORED

Bob Geldof entitled his autobiography *Is That It?*.[5] At one point he had just raised £50 million for Live Aid and, while standing on the stage, he heard a fan shout, "Is that it?" Geldof writes, "It's a question I keep asking myself." In an interview with Mick Brown for *The London Times* newspaper we read this: "Ask Geldof whether he feels that his life is fulfilled, and he snorts with laughter. 'Not at all. I don't know what that would mean. I am unfulfilled as a human being; otherwise, why are these large holes here?' He thumps his chest. 'Everything I do is because I'm frightened of being bored, because I know that's what's down in those holes. I'm frightened of it; it makes me very depressed. So I stay active. Frenetically so, unfortunately. And that "freneticism" keeps me going all the time and allows me to think I'm not wasting time.'"[6]

Barry Humphries, the Australian comedian, entitled his book *More Please*.[7] He writes, "I always wanted more. I never had enough milk or money or socks or sex or holidays or first editions or solitude or gramophone records or free meals or real friends or guiltless pleasure or neckties or applause or unquestioning love... Of course, I have had more than my share of most of these commodities but it always left me with a vague feeling of unfulfillment: where was the rest?"

Isn't it amazing how this theme of discontent, of wanting something more, of being unfulfilled, is predominant in music, film and literature? All around us we see people:

- setting their goals;
- achieving them;
- feeling euphoria for a while;
- and then feeling emptiness all over again.

So they set more goals to fill the emptiness, and the cycle begins again. But there is still something missing. It seems that lasting fulfillment never comes by simply getting what we want. Part of us is still not satisfied.

Thom Yorke, of the band Radiohead, was asked why he continued to make music, even though he'd already achieved the success he hoped for. He said, "It's filling the hole. That's all anyone does." To the question, "What happens to the hole?" Yorke paused a long time before answering: "It's still there."[8]

---

[5] Bob Geldof with Paul Vallely, *Is That it?* (London: Sidgwick & Jackson, 1986).
[6] *The London Times*, September 1998.
[7] Barry Humphries, *More Please* (Middlesex: Viking, 1992), p. xi.
[8] *New Musical Express*, 2001.

In the movie *The Matrix*,[9] Morpheus says to Neo: "Let me tell you why you are here. It's because you know something. What you know you can't explain, but you feel it. You've felt it your entire life. There is something wrong with the world. You don't know what it is but it's there, like a splinter in your mind driving you mad."

Augustine summed up the problem 1,500 years ago when he wrote about God, "you have made us for yourself, and our heart is restless until it rests in you."[10] Could he be right?

Please take the time to find out.

AT THE END OF THE TALK

Let me leave you with the following questions for your groups:

➤ *Display the following questions and read them aloud.*

- **What is *your* view of Christianity?**

- **How do you feel about making time to read Mark?**

➤ *Allow 30 minutes for groups to work together through the* Study Guide *section called GROUP DISCUSSION 2.*

AT THE END OF THE DISCUSSION

This is the "official" end of the evening, although if you want to continue the discussion, you're welcome to do so.

Please take the Bible and *Study Guide* with you. Each week, we'd like you to explore a few chapters of Mark before we meet again. The HOME STUDY section in your *Study Guide* will help you do this. By the end of Week 6, you'll have read through the whole Gospel of Mark.

Thanks again for making time to come. Do work through the HOME STUDY section for Week 1 before next time, and I hope to see you then.

---

9 *The Matrix* (dir. Andy Wachowski and Larry Wachowski; prod. Joel Silver; Warner Brothers, 1999).
10 *Augustine's Confessions*, Book 1 (I). Taken from *Saint Augustine, Confessions* (trans. Henry Chadwick; Oxford: Oxford University Press, 1991), p. 3.

CHRISTIANITY
E✝PLORED

JESUS
- WHO WAS HE?

BEFORE THE TALK

➢ Welcome the course participants and suggest they take 20 minutes to work through the Study Guide section called GROUP DISCUSSION 1 with their group.

THE TALK

➢ Deliver the talk. The wording below is intended only as a general guide. The aim of the talk is to show from Mark's Gospel that Jesus acts with God's power and God's authority. It should challenge participants to trust him to have authority over their lives.

Good evening and welcome to Week 2 of **Christianity Explored**. It's great to see you again.

I hope you can remember what we said last week. It was very simple, yet incredibly important. Christianity is not about beautiful buildings and boring services; it's not about throwing your brain out of the window. It is all about Jesus Christ. That's why we began last week with Mark chapter 1, verse 1: "The beginning of the gospel about Jesus Christ, the Son of God."

The actor Noel Coward was once asked, "What do you think about God?" to which he replied, "We've never been properly introduced."[1]

We saw last week that, according to the Bible, God *has* introduced himself to us through Jesus.

---

[1] Noel Coward, English playwright, actor and composer (1899–1973).

So who was Jesus? Was he a good moral teacher, a Galilean carpenter, a compassionate miracle worker, a great figure of history or what?

We've already seen that Mark's verdict goes far beyond that. Look again at Mark chapter 1, verse 1 on page ..... of the Bible: "The beginning of the gospel about Jesus Christ, the Son of God."

The word "Christ" isn't Jesus' surname; he wouldn't come under "C" in the Nazareth phone book. It means "God's anointed King." Now that was an outrageous thing for Mark to write. Writing such things could get you thrown to the lions, because everyone was supposed to worship the Roman Emperor Nero as the gods' anointed king. But, right at the start, Mark says that there *is* a higher authority than the emperor.

And what Mark does over the first few chapters of his book is stack up layer after layer of evidence to justify his claim that Jesus is the Christ, the Son of God.

➤ *You will need to have the following headings ready for display, gradually revealing each of the headings as the talk progresses.*

Jesus has power and authority:

to teach

over sickness

over nature

over death

to forgive sins

JESUS HAS POWER AND AUTHORITY TO TEACH

So let's look at the first block of evidence. Please turn with me to Mark chapter 1, verses 21–22.

➤ *Read aloud Mark 1:21–22.*

What set Jesus apart from the other teachers of the law was the way he taught. The teachers of the law did not come up with their own material. There was nothing original in their teaching. They never taught without quoting other sources. They hid behind the great rabbis of the past and claimed no authority of their own. But Jesus did not teach like that. He didn't hide behind anybody else's authority; he claimed authority of his own. He said, "I tell you on my authority; you can take it from me."

Jesus not only *claims* that his words have as much authority as God's words; when he speaks, it's as if somebody has suddenly switched on the lights in a dark room. What people heard from the lips of Jesus explained their lives to them. So we see in verse 22 that the people were amazed at his teaching.

But then we have to ask: Was he all talk? Did Jesus actually live out what he taught? And the staggering answer is that he did.

> *I have to say this was the first thing I found so compelling about Jesus. At sixteen I started keeping a diary because I thought I was such a great guy that I owed the world a record of my life. What I found was my own selfishness. Also there was a total contradiction between what I said and did.*

Most of us are aware of our own selfishness and the tension that exists between what we say and what we do. But Jesus was no religious hypocrite. He taught: "Love your enemies and pray for those who persecute you."[2] Later, as he is being killed, he prays for his executioners, "Father, forgive them, for they do not know what they are doing."[3] So Jesus has power and authority to teach.

JESUS HAS POWER AND AUTHORITY OVER SICKNESS

But Jesus wasn't merely a teacher. Please look at chapter 1, verses 29–31.

➤ *Read aloud Mark 1:29–31.*

Here Jesus demonstrates absolute authority over sickness. Just a touch of his hand and the fever is cured. And this is not an isolated incident. Three verses later, in verse 34, we read that Jesus cured whole crowds of sick people. A few days later his touch cured a man with leprosy, the ancient equivalent of AIDS in terms of its severity and the stigma attached to it. Then, in chapter 2, his word healed a paralytic: bones, muscles and tendons knitted together before people's eyes without a hint of surgery.

---

[2] Matthew 5:44.
[3] Luke 23:34.

By verse 12 of chapter 2 everyone is amazed, saying, "We have never seen anything like this!" The deaf hear, the blind see and the lame walk. There are, in fact, thirty healings recorded in the Gospels, all showing us that Jesus has power and authority over sickness.

And you may be interested to know that non-Christian sources of the day also speak of Jesus' healings. Josephus, the Samaritan historian, calls Jesus "a doer of wonderful works."[4] Everybody was talking about his miraculous power – the only debate was where the power came from. So Jesus has power and authority over sickness.

JESUS HAS POWER AND AUTHORITY OVER NATURE

The third block of evidence is in Mark 4, verses 35–41.

➤ *Read aloud Mark 4:35–41*.

Jesus and his followers are in a boat on the Lake of Galilee and, in verse 37, "a furious squall" blows up. Now the word translated "furious squall" actually means whirlwind.

As the waves break over the boat so that it's nearly swamped, Peter and the other hardened fishermen, who have spent their lives on the Lake of Galilee, say to one another, "We're going to die; we're dead."

Now I doubt you would pass the Galilee Lifeboat Safety exams if you said the best course of action in a whirlwind was to call the carpenter. But the disciples do. In their terror they wake Jesus, who was in the stern, sleeping on a cushion. Note the eyewitness detail – he was sleeping on a cushion!

And they say: "Teacher, don't you care if we drown?" What does Jesus do? Grab the helm and steer them out of the whirlwind? No. He gets up and says: "Quiet! Be still!" Immediately, we read in verse 39, the wind dies down and all is completely calm. It normally takes days for waves to calm down, but Jesus flattens them with a few words.

Try it next time you're on a boat in rough seas. I'd make sure you are on your own when you do this, but go out to the back of the boat and say, "Quiet! Be still!"

---

[4] Josephus, *The Antiquities of the Jews*, Book 18, Ch. 39 (3). Taken from *The Genuine Works of Flavius Josephus*, IV (trans. William Whiston; Edinburgh: J. and J. Fairbairn, A. Laurie, and J. Symington, 1793), p. 79.

CHRISTIANITY
E7PLORED

But this is what they saw Jesus doing. No wonder the passage ends in verse 41: "They were terrified and asked each other, 'Who is this? Even the wind and the waves obey him!'" Whoever he is, he has power and authority over nature.

JESUS HAS POWER AND AUTHORITY OVER DEATH

Then, in the next chapter, the disciples witness Jesus doing something even more astonishing. Because in the next chapter we see Jesus demonstrating power and authority over death.

Many people in our culture just block death out of their minds. They are like the poet Siegfried Sassoon, who wrote: "At the age of twenty-two I believed myself to be inextinguishable."[5] The brevity of life doesn't cross their minds. It's easy to feel like that if we've never experienced the death of someone close to us.

> *I was certainly like that until my godfather was suddenly killed when I was a teenager. And I then discovered that death is so painful, so wrenching – not least because it severs relationships with loved ones.*

Loving relationships are so hard to come by. That's why death is so painful, because it severs those relationships.

You may have come across bereavement cards that say things like: "those whom we have loved never really go away." But that's a lie. That's the whole problem. They do go away, and we miss them so much. It is the separation that is so hard to bear.

Well, in the next block of evidence we see Jesus confronting death as its master, with total authority over it. Please turn with me to Mark 5, verses 21–24.

➤ *Read aloud Mark 5:21–24.*

Here we have a religious leader, a synagogue ruler named Jairus, in agony because he is powerless to help his little daughter, who is dying.

Can you identify with this man? Imagine the desperation and powerlessness you would feel if you saw a little nephew, godchild or your own child dying. That is the emotional intensity of this passage.

---

[5] Siegfried Sassoon, English poet and novelist (1886–1967).

Now let's pick up the story again in verse 35.

➤ *Read aloud Mark 5:35–36.*

You can't get more shocking than that. His little daughter is dying and then he hears the terrible words in verse 35, "Your daughter is dead." But Jesus says that he shouldn't worry. Instead, he should just trust him. Now it is a brave man who says something like that to a distraught father. A brave man, or at least one who is supremely confident of his own power.

Let's see what happens next. Look at verse 37.

➤ *Read aloud Mark 5:37–42.*

Jesus takes the corpse by the hand and says, "Little girl, get up!" And the father is reunited with the daughter he thought he'd lost forever. The message is clear: it is as easy for Jesus to raise a person from the dead as it is for us to wake somebody from sleep.

Jesus has power and authority over death. And not just over the death of a little girl but also over our deaths and his own, as we'll see over the next few weeks.

And if he does indeed have power over death, then it is insanity to ignore him, to say, "I'm just not interested," or "This is boring," or "That's fine for you to believe." One day you and I are going to die. The question is: would you be prepared to trust Jesus with your own death?

JESUS HAS POWER AND AUTHORITY TO FORGIVE SINS

But I have to tell you that "Quiet, be still!" and "Get up!" are not the most outrageous things Jesus says. Please turn back to chapter 2, verses 1–12, for Mark's fifth block of evidence – the passage we've just looked at briefly in our GROUP DISCUSSION.

➤ *Read aloud Mark 2:1–7.*

I can't imagine what the owner of the house thought as his roof was ripped open. But what is extraordinary here are Jesus' words to the paralytic in verse 5: "Son, your sins are forgiven."

Why on earth does Jesus say *that* rather than immediately curing the man of his paralysis?

Well, we can only grasp this if we understand what the word "sin" means.

A few years ago, *The Independent* newspaper ran an article on the seven deadly sins. And the writer said: "In this day and age, sin has lost its sting. A bit of sinning is much more likely to be seen as a spot of grown-up naughtiness, the kind of thing that sends a delicious shock through the system."[6]

That's what many people think of sin. It's not very serious. It's a bit of fun on the side. But rightly understood, in the way that the Bible describes sin, there is nothing nice about it. Jesus is saying that sin is humankind's biggest problem. It's not paralysis, or global warming, or terrorism, but sin.

Sin is not just doing naughty things. It is not just lust or laziness or whatever. No, according to the Bible, sin is ignoring God in the world he has made. It's rebelling against him by living without reference to him.

We may not have committed adultery or murder, but we have all said, "I will decide exactly how I live my life."

Now why is ignoring God in his world so serious? It's because if I insist on my independence in a world that God has made, then that has consequences. The Bible clearly links sin with death – and not just death here, but eternal death. That's why sin matters. And we'll be looking more at those consequences next week.

The staggering claim that Jesus makes in this passage is that he has authority to forgive sin.

The implications of this are not lost on the religious leaders. They don't mind the paralytic being called a sinner; they know everyone's a sinner. Their problem with Jesus is shown in verse 7: "Why does this fellow talk like that? He's blaspheming! Who can forgive sins but God alone?"

They are saying to Jesus, "Who do you think you are that you can forgive sin?" Sin offends God. So only God has the right to forgive it. The question is: does Jesus really have the authority to forgive sin, or is he blaspheming as the religious leaders claim?

To answer that question, Jesus does something amazing. Let's read from verse 8.

➤ *Read aloud Mark 2:8–12.*

---

6 *The Independent*, 18 December 1990.

As if to substantiate his claim to have God's authority and power, Jesus immediately cures the man's paralysis with a few words. The crowd that has crammed into this house to see Jesus is totally amazed.

But the healing is not an end in itself. Jesus doesn't do it with a flourish as if performing magic tricks at a circus. No, he cures this man – and countless others – in order to reveal his true identity. He is quite obviously acting with God's authority and God's power. And he expects us to draw the obvious conclusion.

As Jesus teaches, calms the storm, raises the dead, heals the sick and forgives sins he acts in God's world with God's authority.

Of course, if this is true, then it's not just an abstract idea. It gets very personal. Do I recognize who he is? Will I recognize that he is my teacher, whether I like it or not? Do I recognize that he has authority over my death, whether I like it or not? Do I see that he has the authority to forgive my sin or leave it unforgiven? These are good questions to ask – because if Jesus is who he claims to be, then it is a scandal that we haven't lived under his authority.

AT THE END OF THE TALK

Let me leave you with the following questions for your groups:

➤ *Display the following questions and read them aloud.*

> • **What is your view of Jesus?**
>
> • **What do you think of the five blocks of evidence Mark gives us?**

➤ *Allow 30 minutes for groups to work together through the* Study Guide *section called GROUP DISCUSSION 2.*

AT THE END OF THE DISCUSSION

Please feel free to continue your discussions, but this is the "official" end of the evening. Before next time, use the HOME STUDY section in your *Study Guide* to help you as you continue to read through Mark.

CHRISTIANITY
E✝PLORED

JESUS
- WHY DID HE COME?

BEFORE THE TALK

➤ Welcome the course participants and suggest they take 20 minutes to work through the Study Guide section called *GROUP DISCUSSION 1* with their group.

THE TALK

➤ *Deliver the talk. The wording below is intended only as a general guide. The aim of the talk is to show that Jesus came to rescue us from sin, judgement and hell (Mark 2:17).*

Sometimes we experience things in life that give us an uncomfortable dose of reality. Maybe you've joined a gym and discovered just how unfit you are; or had a medical check that gave you a jolt; or been told a few home truths by a close friend.

> When I joined my university rugby club, I was sent a summer training schedule and told to show up for club pre-season testing on 12 September, just before term started. I circled the date on my calendar but filed the training schedule in the bin, thinking, "Well, I'll just go on some runs and do a few sit-ups. I'll be fine." Anyway, when I arrived, the coach came in and said, "Right, we'll start with the Bleep Test." This was a test in which you had to run back and forth over twenty yards in time with a bleep that gets faster and faster. You ran until you dropped. I was the second to drop out, having collapsed and been physically sick. Then we had to strip off to our shorts for the fat tests. There was only one other player with a higher percentage of body fat than me. Everything was carefully noted down. It was extremely humiliating. At the end of all these tests the coach said, "Well, it's not comfortable,

but at least we've discovered the truth on the training ground before the real questions get asked out on the playing field. Some of you have really been exposed, haven't you?"

Listening to what Jesus has to say about you and me can be extremely uncomfortable because it exposes what we are really like. And, in a way, the title for tonight's talk could be, "I wish I didn't have to tell you this!"

Last week we asked, "Who was Jesus?" Whatever answer we come up with, it has to take into account the evidence in Mark's Gospel, evidence that suggests he is a man with God's power and authority.

He amazed crowds with his teaching, cured diseases and calmed a storm, as we just saw in our GROUP DISCUSSION. We've seen him raising the dead, saying, "Little girl, I say to you, get up!" and bringing a corpse back to life. And we've also seen him forgiving sin, as you will remember from the story of the paralytic at the end of last week.

Tonight we turn our attention to another vital question: "Why did Jesus come?" How would you answer that?

Did he want to bring peace on earth? That's the Jesus of Christmas carols. Was it to cure disease and end the sufferings of the world? That's Jesus the great healer. Or did he want to reform society and give us an example of how to live? That's Jesus the great teacher.

Although there is an element of truth in each of those options, Mark's Gospel doesn't give any of them as Jesus' main aim. According to Mark, the reason Jesus came was to rescue rebels.

➤ *You will need to have the following headings ready for display, gradually revealing each of the headings as the talk progresses.*

Jesus came to rescue rebels

We are all rebels

We are in danger

JESUS CAME TO RESCUE REBELS

So, point 1, Jesus came to rescue rebels.

Please open your Bibles to Mark chapter 2, verses 13–17.

➤ *Read aloud Mark 2:13–17.*

You will see in this passage that there are two groups of people – the good guys and the bad guys. The bad guys are made up of people like Levi. Tax collectors were more hated then than they are today. Not only were they seen as cheating their fellow Jews out of their hard-earned cash, but they were also seen as betraying God's people because they were working for the occupying Roman forces.

The good guys are the senior religious figures of the day – the teachers of the law and the Pharisees. They looked impeccable – whiter than white, in religious terms.

The question is, who would you expect Jesus to hang around with? Instinctively we'd expect him to want to be with the good guys, the religious elite.

But this is what Jesus says to them, "It is not the healthy who need a doctor, but the sick. I have not come to call the righteous, but sinners."

The big shock at this dinner party is who Jesus wants on his guest list. In verse 17 Jesus says, "I'm a doctor and, as a doctor, I'm interested in the sick because the sick know they need me." It's obvious, isn't it, that doctors don't dish out medicine to the healthy? If a doctor came into your office with his scalpel and pills, you'd say, "Get lost, don't come around here trying to carve me up. Go and slice up some sick person instead." So Jesus says here, "If you think you're righteous, if you think you're healthy, then you won't think that you need me. Just as healthy people don't need doctors, so people who think they are righteous don't need me."

"No," says Jesus here, "I've come for sinners. I've come for people who realize they are living as rebels in God's world." That's what a sinner is – someone who knows he has not let God be God. Jesus makes it quite clear here that he is interested in people who realize they're bad, not in people who think they are good.

So, the qualification for coming to Jesus is not, "Are you good enough?" but, "Are you bad enough?" He's come for sinners, not the righteous.

So that's the answer to the question, "Why did Jesus come?" He came to call sinners. "I've come," Jesus says, "on a rescue mission to call rebels back into a relationship with the God who made them, with the God who gives them each breath, and yet who is treated like a footnote in their lives."

We'll see how Jesus achieves that rescue next week, but tonight I want to focus on the assumption that Jesus is making. He is assuming that we are all rebels who need to be rescued, even if we believe we're righteous. Jesus assumes that you and I need him to rescue us.

WE ARE ALL REBELS

And that's the second point: we are all rebels.

Jesus is, after all, being a little sarcastic when he calls the teachers of the law and the Pharisees "righteous" in verse 17. They are righteous by their own standards, but not by God's. Actually they are totally self-righteous, and just as much in need of rescue as everyone else, even though they don't see it. In fact, as we discover in Mark chapter 3, verse 6, these "righteous" people end up wanting to kill Jesus.

Jesus assumes here that every single human being needs to be rescued. And if that assumption is uncomfortable for you, then we need to expose ourselves to another tough question: What is the world really like? Surely, when we look at the world, we see a mixture of good and evil.

There are lots of things about the world that we love – things that make life worth living. Seeing some things makes us think that this world is a pretty special place. We see a little child leap with delight into his mother's arms. Or a couple strolling along holding hands, lost in each other's company.

But then, the child falls down and starts crying, and we realize that pain is never far behind happiness in our world. Then we see the couple fighting and think of all the marriages that end in divorce.

A history of the twentieth century will tell you that one hundred million people died violently in those one hundred years. That's more than died violently in the previous nineteen centuries put together. It doesn't take much to realize that war and death are never far behind peace and life in our world.

The Bible says that the reason *the world* is not the way it's supposed to be is because *we* are not the way *we're* supposed to be.

CHRISTIANITY
E✝PLORED

And yet it still grates against our pride to think that we need to be rescued. We might concede that *some* people need to be rescued: the really evil people – the murderers, rapists, the paedophiles – but not us, and certainly not our family and friends. We're basically good people with a few human faults here and there. We're confident that our good points outweigh the bad – that we are good enough for God. But we must ask the next tough question: "What are we really like?"

Imagine for a moment that this room is a public gallery, and plastered all over the walls is a record of your life. Every day is on the walls: 24 May 1989, 24 May 1990, 24 May 1991, 24 May 1999 – every single day. It is a complete and true account not only of everything you've ever said and done, but also of everything you've ever thought. Even your motives are revealed for everyone to see.

Now I'm sure there would be lots to celebrate on those walls: loving relationships, real achievements, acts of kindness, moments of generosity and selflessness, perhaps a flourishing career. But there would also be thousands of things that we'd want to keep out of the public gaze. Which bit of the wall would you most want to cover up? Which day? Maybe it's something no-one knows – not even your closest friend or your spouse.

And it is not just the things we've said and done that are a problem. The things we *should* have said and the things we *should* have done are up on the walls as well. Everything is exposed for everyone to see.

If my life was on the walls it would be a nightmare. I wouldn't be able to stay in the room, I'd be so ashamed. Could you – if you're being honest?

So what's the problem? Jesus gives us the answer in Mark chapter 7.

The issue in this chapter is what makes someone unclean in God's eyes; what makes someone unacceptable to God. The Pharisees are blaming external things – you are unacceptable because of what you touch, where you go, what you eat. But Jesus says the problem is much closer to home.

Please turn to Mark chapter 7, and we'll read verses 18–23.

➤ *Read aloud Mark 7:18–23.*

The problem, says Jesus in verse 21, is our hearts. That's what makes us unclean. If we were to trace all of the evil in the world back to its source, the place we'd end up is the human heart.

Why do we find it hard to do the right thing? Why is it so difficult to keep good relationships good? Why do we hurt the people we love the most? Why can't we automatically love each other? Because we've all got a heart problem.

Out of our hearts come evil thoughts, sexual immorality, theft, murder, adultery, greed, malice, deceit, lewdness, envy, slander, arrogance and folly. Those things are what make us unclean.

"But," you may be saying to yourself, "I'm not that bad. I know I'm not perfect, but I'm not as bad that." Well, it gets worse, I'm afraid. Please turn to Mark chapter 12 and we'll read verses 28–30.

➤ *Read aloud Mark 12:28–30.*

Since God made us, and sustains us, and gives us every good thing we enjoy, and since he has power and authority over our lives, how should we respond to him? Jesus tells us: our response should be to love him.

And the really scary word here is "all" – love God with *all* your heart, soul, mind and strength. So no part of our lives should be withheld from God. He is to have all of everything.

But actually he's had all of nothing.

We decide exactly what we will do with our heart, soul, mind and strength. We give our hearts to lots of things, but not to our Creator. We don't even *know* his commands, let alone seek to obey them. We develop relationships with others, but we neglect the very relationship for which we were primarily designed.

And instead of *loving* God, we live as if we *were* God. If we think about everything up on those walls, the complete record of our lives, that's true, isn't it? Each and every one of us is guilty – guilty of rebelling against our loving Creator. That rebellion is what the Bible calls "sin."

And that leads us to point 3. Because of our sin, we're in danger.

CHRISTIANITY
EXPLORED

I'm sure many of you have seen the movie *Titanic*.[1] Most of the passengers are blind to how serious their situation is. They are having the party of their lives. But the shipbuilder who designed the boat knows the truth. He knows that the ship will sink and that there aren't enough lifeboats. He knows the situation is deadly serious.

And Jesus warns us that *our* situation is deadly serious because of our sin. He spells this out very clearly in Mark chapter 9, verses 43–47. And it's not comfortable reading.

➤ *Read aloud Mark 9:43–47.*

Jesus warns us here that our sin will lead us to hell. If we reject God throughout our lives, then ultimately he will respect that decision – and reject us.

Believe me, I take no pleasure in relating these words of Christ, just as God takes no pleasure in allowing people to go their own self-destructive way. I hope you can see that the reason Jesus warns us about hell is because he loves us and does not want us to go there.

According to Jesus, we should do anything we can to avoid going to hell. If our foot causes us to sin, we should cut it off. If it's our eye, we should cut it out. Hell is real, and we should do anything we can to avoid it.

But here's our predicament. What's our biggest problem? *It is our heart*. If our problem was the foot, or the hand, we could cut it off. But we can't cut out our heart.

That, above all else, is why we need Jesus to rescue us. That's why he came. As he said himself, "I have not come to call the righteous, but sinners."

And next week, we'll see exactly how Jesus does that.

---

[1] *Titanic* (dir. James Cameron; prod. James Cameron and Jon Landau; Paramount Pictures, 1997).

AT THE END OF THE TALK

Let me leave you with the following questions for your groups:

➤ *Display the following questions and read them aloud.*

> * **Do you agree that you're in danger?**
>
> * **How would you feel if your every thought, word and action was displayed on the walls for everyone to see?**
>
> * **What's your reaction to Jesus' words in Mark chapter 9, verses 43–47?**

➤ *Allow 30 minutes for groups to work together through the* Study Guide *section called GROUP DISCUSSION 2.*

AT THE END OF THE DISCUSSION

Before next time, use the HOME STUDY section in your *Study Guide* to help you as you continue to read through Mark.

CHRISTIANITY
E⨉PLORED

JESUS

- HIS DEATH

BEFORE THE TALK

➤ Welcome the course participants and suggest they take 20 minutes to work through the Study Guide section called GROUP DISCUSSION 1 with their group.

THE TALK

➤ Deliver the talk. The wording below is intended only as a general guide. The aim of the talk is to explain the significance of the cross, and explore the different reactions to Jesus' death as described in Mark's Gospel.

> I was once in Australia staying with a friend, and he took me to a beach on Botany Bay. The beach was empty, the sun was out and the water was crystal blue and as calm as a millpond. So I decided I had to go for a swim. I was just taking my shirt off, when my host said, "What are you doing?" I said, "I'm going for a swim." He said, "But what about these signs?" I looked around and saw a huge sign that read: "Danger – Sharks. No swimming." I said, "Oh, don't be ridiculous, I'll be fine." He looked at me and said, "Listen, mate, two hundred Australians have been killed by sharks over the years. You have to work out whether those signs are there to save you or to ruin your fun. You're of age – you decide." And with that he walked off, up the beach. Well, I just sat there and rather sheepishly put my shirt back on. I hope you see my point. Jesus' words are like a huge danger sign for us. We are free to decide whether to ignore it or not, but he warns us for a reason.

Last week we saw that, according to Jesus, each of us has a serious "heart problem." In Mark chapter 7, verse 20 he says this: "What comes out of a man is what makes him 'unclean' [by "unclean" Jesus means "sinful"]. For from within, out of men's hearts, come evil thoughts, sexual immorality, theft, murder, adultery," and so the list goes on. This means that we're all in danger, whether we realize it or not, because ultimately our sin will lead us to hell.

But as we also saw, the wonderful news is that Jesus does not want us to go there. As he said himself: "I have not come to call the righteous but sinners." He wants to rescue sinful people like you and me. The question is: how does Jesus do that?

Turn with me to Mark chapter 8, verse 31.

➤ *Read aloud Mark 8:31.*

So Jesus taught his followers that he *must* suffer and be rejected. It was something he had to do. But why?

We get the answer in Mark chapter 10, verse 45, where Jesus tells us this:

➤ *Read aloud Mark 10:45.*

So that's what Jesus says he came to do, "to give his life as a ransom for many." Jesus went to his death willingly and deliberately. In fact, he knew it was necessary.

> *I recently looked at a biography of Winston Churchill and it was interesting to see that in over three hundred pages only three were about Churchill's death.*

If you look at most biographies, the writers want to talk about the person's life, not their death. In fact, their deaths are often glossed over. And yet, one *third* of each Gospel talks about Jesus' death.

Not only that, but Christians never stop talking about the cross. This seems strange because crucifixion, the manner in which Jesus died, was considered terribly shameful. The ancient Roman writer Cicero described it like this: "But the executioner, the veil that covers the condemned man's head, the cross of crucifixion, these are horrors which ought to be far removed not only from the person of a Roman citizen, but even from his thoughts and his gaze and his hearing. It is utterly wrong that a Roman citizen, a free man, would ever be compelled to endure or tolerate such dreadful things."[1]

---

[1] From Cicero's speech in defence of Gaius Rabirius who was charged with high treason, *In Defence of Rabirius*, V.16. Taken from Michael Grant, *Cicero Murder Trials* (Middlesex: Penguin, 1975).

CHRISTIANITY
E✝PLORED

Crucifixion was deliberately made cruel and gruesome so that any slave considering rebellion would pass by the crucified victim and conclude that it could never be worth the risk. It was the ultimate deterrent.

So why has the cross become the universally-recognized symbol of Christianity? Christians could have chosen a manger to remind them of Jesus' birth, or perhaps a scroll to remind them of his amazing teaching. But no, it's a cross – a reminder of his death. And certainly no other religion celebrates the death of its founder.

The answer is simple. The cross is so important because Jesus' death is the only way we can be saved from our sin. It is how Jesus rescues people. To understand exactly what that means, we need to read an account of Jesus' death, so let's look at Mark chapter 15, verses 22 to 39.

➤ *Read aloud Mark 15:22–39.*

We learn three striking things from that passage:

➤ *Display the following headings and read them aloud.*

God was angry

Jesus was abandoned

We can be accepted

GOD WAS ANGRY

Firstly, God was angry. Verse 33 states: "At the sixth hour darkness came over the whole land until the ninth hour."

Mark is counting hours according to the Jewish system, so the sixth hour would have been noon. At the moment when the midday sun should have been at its brightest in the sky, a darkness fell over the whole land and remained until three in the afternoon. It could not have been an eclipse, because Passover always fell on a full moon and a solar eclipse is out of the question during a full moon. And, don't forget, solar eclipses never last more than about six minutes. This darkness lasted three hours. So, something supernatural is going on.

Time and again in the Bible, light symbolizes God's presence and blessing, while darkness is a sign of God's anger and judgement. So when darkness comes over the land as Jesus dies, we know right away that God is angry.

Now, we won't understand this if we see anger as something that is unpredictable and wild, the product of a quick temper. God's anger is not like that. It is his settled, controlled, personal hostility to all that is wrong. And a God who cares about injustice is right to be angry about sin, and right to punish it.

God is a God of holiness, of blazing purity, and he hates what is evil. When it comes to evil he doesn't lean back in a rocking chair and pretend nothing has happened. No, evil matters to God. So lying matters to God, as does selfishness. Likewise, adultery matters to him. Greed matters to him. Murder matters. The deaths of Kosovan women and children because they are from the wrong ethnic group matter to God, as do the deaths of those in the World Trade Center, and he will not simply overlook them. Surely if we care about the injustices we see in the world, we cannot expect our loving Creator to care any the less.

So, as Jesus was dying on the cross, darkness came over the whole land. God was acting in anger to punish sin. But that leaves us with a question: whose sin was God angry at? The staggering answer is that God seems to be angry at Jesus.

JESUS WAS ABANDONED

That brings us to our second heading: Jesus was abandoned. Verse 34 says: "And at the ninth hour Jesus cried out in a loud voice, *'Eloi, Eloi, lama sabachthani?'* which means, 'My God, My God, why have you forsaken me?'"

Now there is no doubt that Jesus suffered physical agony on the cross, but what is being spoken of here is spiritual agony – being forsaken by God. And the word Jesus uses for "God" here is *"Eloi."* Normally Jesus uses the word *"Abba,"* which is close to our word "Daddy." But *"Eloi"* has none of that warmth or intimacy.

On the cross, Jesus was abandoned by God. It was Jesus that God was punishing. But Jesus had led a sinless life. Not even his fiercest enemies could find any fault with him. So why should God be punishing him? And why has Jesus allowed himself to be subjected to this?

Answer: so that we can be rescued. How can this be?

➤ *Hold a blank video tape in your right hand.*

I'd like you to pretend that this video is a record of your life. The Bible says: "Nothing in all creation is hidden from God's sight. Everything is uncovered and laid bare before the eyes of him to whom we must give account."[2] So everything that we've ever done, said and thought is on this video. Now the first thing I want to say is that there's lots of stuff on here that's great. Perhaps there's a loving home, selfless acts, academic achievements, success in the arts or on the sports field, there might be a flourishing career.

But there is also a lot on this video that you're ashamed of. Things you'd rather people didn't see. Sir Arthur Conan Doyle, the creator of Sherlock Holmes, sent a telegram to the twelve most respectable people in London as a joke one night. The telegram read: "Flee – all is revealed." Within 24 hours, six of the twelve had left the country.[3]

Like them, we all have secrets that we would hate to have exposed. But the Bible tells us that it's all recorded. And not just the way we've treated others, but the way we've treated God is also recorded. The Bible's way of describing what's on the video is "the unfavourable record of our debts."[4]

Now let's suppose that my left hand represents me,

➤ *Hold out your left hand, palm uppermost.*

and the ceiling represents God. The Bible says that between us and God is this "record of our debts," and it separates us from God.

➤ *Place the video on the upturned palm of your left hand.*

In fact, the Bible says that God is so pure, that even if only one second of my life were recorded on this video, it would be enough to separate me from God. My sin cuts me off from God; I am utterly forsaken. But let me illustrate what happens at the cross.

➤ *Hold out your right hand, palm uppermost. Your left hand should still have the video on it.*

---

2 Hebrews 4:13.
3 Sir Arthur Conan Doyle, writer (1859–1930).
4 Good News Bible, Colossians 2:14.

Suppose that my right hand represents Jesus, and remember that the ceiling represents God. As Jesus hung on the cross there was no barrier between him and God. He always perfectly obeyed the will of God. But, while Jesus was on the cross, he took my sin.

➤ *Now transfer the video from the left hand to the right, upturned hand.*

That's why Jesus cried out, "My God, my God, why have you forsaken me?" as he hung on the cross. It couldn't have been *his* sin that made him feel separated from God, because the Bible tells us that Jesus was free from sin. No, it was our sin that separated him from God. In those agonizing moments, Jesus was taking upon himself all the punishment that our sin, everything on this video, deserves. The Bible says "we all, like sheep, have gone astray, each of us has turned to his own way; but the LORD has laid on him the iniquity of us all."[5] Jesus died as my substitute, in my place, taking the punishment I deserve.

➤ *Refer people back to your left hand, now empty, with your palm upturned.*

The result of Jesus' extraordinary self-sacrifice is simply this: we can be accepted by God. Jesus paid the price for sin so that we never have to. The amazing truth is that Jesus loved me enough to die for my sin. He died for my sin, and for the sin of everyone who puts their trust in him.

WE CAN BE ACCEPTED

And this leads us to the third point: We can be accepted.

Let's look again at verses 37 and 38.

➤ *Read aloud Mark 15:37–38.*

Now, here Mark records the exact moment of Jesus' death, but then he turns our attention to something that happens simultaneously at the temple, which is on the other side of the city. He wants us to understand that the two events are connected in some way.

When Jesus dies, the thirty-foot high curtain in the temple, which was as thick as the span of a man's hand, was torn from top to bottom. Why is that significant? Well,

---

5 Isaiah 53:6.

this thick curtain used to hang in the temple, dividing the people from the place where God was said to live. The curtain was like a big "Do Not Enter" sign. It said loudly and clearly that it is impossible for sinful people like you and me to walk into God's presence.

Then, suddenly, as Jesus dies on the cross, God rips this curtain in two, from top to bottom. It's as if God is saying: "The way is now open for people to approach me." And that's only possible because Jesus has just paid the price for our sin.

And it's not as if Jesus is some innocent third party, being picked on by God. As Paul says in Colossians chapter 1 verse 19, "God was pleased to have all his fulness dwell in [Jesus]." The remarkable truth is that God himself is making peace with us by willingly sacrificing himself.

Mark's description of Jesus' death focuses not only on Jesus, but also on the reactions of those who witness his death. And it's interesting to see how they respond.

➤ *You will need to have the following headings ready for display, gradually revealing each of the headings as the talk progresses.*

Reactions to the cross:

the busy soldiers
the self-satisfied religious leaders
the cowardly Pontius Pilate
the detached bystander
the Roman centurion, who recognized that Jesus was "the Son of God"

THE BUSY SOLDIERS

To begin with there are the soldiers, responsible for carrying out the execution. We first meet the soldiers in Mark 15, verses 16–20.

➤ *Read aloud Mark 15:16–20.*

And this is how they react to the cross in verse 24.

➤ *Read aloud Mark 15:24.*

For these soldiers, the main legacy of the cross is Jesus' clothes. They are absorbed in just doing their job. They see nothing special about this man. They'd seen it all before. No doubt they did their job well but, in doing their duty, they missed the true legacy of the cross.

Many go through life doing their duty, working hard, saving for the mortgage. Intent on their day-to-day activities, they are too busy to notice what the cross means for them.

THE SELF-SATISFIED RELIGIOUS LEADERS

The second group of people to witness the crucifixion is the religious leaders. Mark tells us that they mock Jesus among themselves. Look at what they say in verses 31–32.

➤ *Read aloud Mark 15:31–32.*

These self-righteous religious leaders are convinced that they know the way to God, and Jesus Christ is not a part of that route. As far as they're concerned, they already have a relationship with God. They already consider themselves to be spiritual people, and they certainly see no need for the cross.

It is often those people, who have created their own religion with their own formula of religious or moral observance, who are the most vicious enemies of the cross.

THE COWARDLY PONTIUS PILATE

And then there's Pontius Pilate.

He orders a sign to be attached to the cross. It reads: THE KING OF THE JEWS. All the Gospel writers assure us that Pilate was convinced of Jesus' innocence. He offers to release Jesus, but the crowd want a man called Barabbas released instead. Time and again, Pilate sticks up for Jesus. But eventually he hands Jesus over to be crucified. So why does Pilate hand over an innocent man? Look at verse 15.

➤ *Read aloud Mark 15:15.*

Pilate was a crowd-pleaser. Although he knew that Jesus was innocent, peer pressure caused him to lose his nerve and made him give in to the evil desires of others. Here was a coward who abandoned Jesus. When he faces a world that despises Jesus, his good intentions are overcome.

CHRISTIANITY
E✝PLORED

THE DETACHED BYSTANDER

Mark also records the reaction of some other bystanders. They hear Jesus cry out and think he's calling to Elijah. In Jewish legend Elijah, who was an Old Testament prophet, was celebrated as a helper of those in need. Then Mark records the reaction of one man in particular. He says this in verse 36:

➤ *Read aloud Mark 15:36.*

This man has just come for the show. He wants to see Elijah perform some spectacular miracle and rescue Jesus. The sight of Jesus on the cross doesn't move him at all. Instead, he is totally detached and refuses to get involved.

There are lots of people like that. They know about the cross, they come to church at Christmas and Easter for the show, but they don't see that Jesus' death affects them personally.

By showing us all these different reactions, it's as if Mark is saying, "OK, this is how others responded to what happened at the cross. What about you? What will you make of the cross?"

Are we too busy like the soldiers? Too self-satisfied like the religious leaders? Too cowardly like Pilate? Or are we too detached like the bystander?

There is, however, one other possible response to the cross.

THE ROMAN CENTURION, WHO RECOGNIZED THAT
JESUS WAS "THE SON OF GOD"

Mark records it for us in verse 39. It's the reaction of a Roman centurion, a hard-bitten soldier who was a high-ranking military officer. He had doubtless fought in many campaigns and seen many men die, but he had never seen a man die like this. This is how Mark describes it:

➤ *Read aloud Mark 15:39.*

And that is our final option as we look at what happened at the cross. We can recognize that Jesus is telling the truth: that he is indeed the Son of God.

If you look across the skyline in London you can see the Old Bailey, the home of British justice. On top of it is Pomeroy's magnificent golden statue of the goddess Justicia holding the scales of justice in one hand and the sword of wrath in the other. She is blindfolded, unable to show partiality, and the message is clear: if we are found to be guilty, then the sword of judgement must fall.

But just across the London skyline, on top of St. Paul's Cathedral, is another golden symbol. It is a cross – a powerful reminder that the sword of God's judgement did fall. But it fell on Jesus Christ.

So what will you do with your sin? Will you take it to the cross to be forgiven or will you take it with you to the grave and to the judgement that must fall?

AT THE END OF THE TALK

Let me leave you with the following questions for your groups:

➤ *Display the following questions and read them aloud.*

- **Can you identify with any of the reactions to Jesus' death on the cross?**

- **Jesus said he came "to give his life as a ransom for many" (Mark 10:45). How do you feel about that?**

➤ *Allow 30 minutes for groups to work together through the* Study Guide *section called GROUP DISCUSSION 2.*

AT THE END OF THE DISCUSSION

Before next time, use the HOME STUDY section in your *Study Guide* to help you as you continue to read through Mark.

➤ *Tell participants that there will be a weekend or day away in a few weeks. Give them a brief idea of what will happen, and ask them to block out the time.*

CHRISTIANITY
E⳨PLORED

WHAT IS GRACE?

BEFORE THE TALK

➤ *Welcome the course participants and suggest they take 20 minutes to work through the* Study Guide *section called GROUP DISCUSSION 1 with their group.*

THE TALK

➤ *Deliver the talk. The wording below is intended only as a general guide. The aim of the talk is to explain God's grace and its implications.*

Please turn with me to Mark chapter 1, verse 1. "The beginning of the gospel [the good news] about Jesus Christ, the Son of God." We've started to explore exactly why Mark describes Jesus as "good news." We've seen who Jesus is: that he has the power and authority of God himself. We've seen what he came to do: to rescue sinners like you and me by dying for us on the cross.

This week let me begin by asking you to jot down your answer to the following question. It's similar to the question the man asks Jesus in the passage we've just looked at in our GROUP DISCUSSION.

➤ *Display the following question and read it aloud.*

> • **If you were to die tonight and God asked, "Why should I let you into heaven?" what would you say?**

Take 2 minutes to jot down your answer.

➤ *Allow 2 minutes for participants to write down their answers.*

Sorry to be morbid, but if you *were* to die tonight and you found yourself standing before God and he asked, "Why should I let you into heaven?" what would you say?

According to the Bible, answers to this question always fall neatly into one of two categories: "the right answer," or "the wrong answer."

Let's look at the wrong answers first. The wrong answer is one that places confidence in what *I am*, or *what I have done*. So if you've written, "God, you should let me in to heaven *because I*...," I'm afraid you're on the wrong track.

➤ *You will need to have each of the following wrong answers written out in big letters on separate pieces of paper. Hold each of them up as you read them.*

Perhaps you've written something like, "Let me in God because I've been pretty good on the whole...

- I'm a good person,
- I don't steal,
- I don't lie (well, not unless I absolutely have to),
- I give to charity,
- I've certainly never killed anyone (Actually, there are *lots* of people worse than I am),
- I pay my taxes,
- I don't drive through red lights,
...Other people like having me around, God, so I imagine you will too."

They sound like reasonable answers.

➤ *Rip the papers in two.*

But I can assure you that none of these things are of any use at all when it comes to entering heaven.

➤ *You will need to have each of the following wrong answers written out in big letters on separate pieces of paper. Hold each of them up as you read them.*

Another wrong answer is the religious one. You may be relying on your religious habits to get you into heaven. So perhaps you've written something like this: "God, you should let me in because...

- I go to church,
- I never take your name in vain (and when others do, I strongly disapprove),
- I do good things in the community,
- I've been baptized,
- I go to communion,
- I sing in the choir,
- I pray *and* read the Bible,

…And there aren't many people you can say that about in this day and age."

You're correct that you're in a minority. But the religious answers are still wrong.

➤ *Rip the papers in two.*

If you *have* written something like that, then let me say to you categorically that doing these religious things will *not* enable you to enter heaven. Again and again, Jesus taught that religious observance has no power to save people. If you are putting your confidence here, then please don't because you've been misled.

In fact, *any* answer which places confidence in what *I am*, or *what I have done* is absolutely useless. Answers that begin "God, you should let me into heaven because I…" will do you no good at all.

Now, there's nothing wrong with those things in themselves. It's good when people try to live honest, selfless lives. But the good things *we do* won't get us into heaven. Why? Because they can't solve the problem of our sin.

Remember what Jesus said in Mark chapter 7, verses 20–23. Let's read them again.

➤ *Read aloud Mark 7:20–23.*

The good things we do count for nothing before God, because our key problem lies deep down in our hearts. When Jesus talks about the heart he's not simply talking about the pump that sends blood around the body. He's referring to the very core of your being – the source of all your urges and instincts, desires and dreams.

Jesus says we are to "Love the Lord our God with all our heart and with all our soul and with all our mind and with all our strength." But that's not the way we live. So our good deeds, whatever they may be, are fine in themselves – but they're no good at solving the problem that keeps us from God: our sin.

According to Jesus, our biggest problem is what we *are*, deep down in our hearts. We are sinful. And nothing *we do* can change that. Our good deeds are like Band-Aids or sticking plasters: they might cover up what we're really like, but they are powerless to actually *cure* us.

Again, I want to stress that there is nothing wrong with good deeds. They only become dangerous when, like the Pharisees and teachers of the law in Mark, I delude myself into thinking that God will accept me because of them.

You see, these religious authorities had already decided the criteria by which God would accept them. They kept their own rules and traditions. Getting God to accept them meant attending to *external* details: for example, they were to wash in special ways and avoid eating certain things. It was all about outward ritual, and nothing to do with our inner problem: the selfishness of the human heart. That's why Jesus says this about them: "These people honour me with their lips, but their hearts are far from me. They worship me in vain; their teachings are but rules taught by men."[1] It is so much easier to concentrate on the outside appearance, to stick on a few Band-Aids, rather than face up to what is within, and Jesus insists that no amount of religious tradition or morality or Bible-reading or "turning over of new leaves" can bring our hearts any closer to God.

Because out of our hearts come "evil thoughts, sexual immorality, theft, murder, adultery, greed, malice, deceit, lewdness, envy, slander, arrogance and folly." Let's be honest about our own hearts here, and try to apply the words on this list to ourselves. Let me ask you this:

• What would it be like never ever to have lied?

• What would it be like never to have nurtured bitterness and hatred?

• What would it be like never to have gossiped?

• What would it be like never to have been selfish or greedy?

• What would it be like never to have entered into a conversation in which our whole purpose was to promote ourselves before others, even if we do it very subtly?

• What would it be like never to have nurtured dirty thoughts?

• What would it be like never to feel vindictive or a little jealous when you hear of another person's success? As the author Gore Vidal admitted: "Whenever a friend succeeds, a little something in me dies."[2]

---

[1] Mark 7:6–7.
[2] *The Sunday Times Magazine*, 6 September 1973.

CHRISTIANITY
E✝PLORED

And what would it be like – on the positive side – to have always loved God with all our heart, soul, mind and strength? What would it be like to have always loved other people as ourselves?

Even Paul, one of the most effective Christian workers in history, lamented the state of his heart when he wrote in Romans chapter 7, verse 19: "For what I do is not the good I want to do: no, the evil I do not want to do – this I keep on doing." Jesus' words about the evil of the human heart are as true for Paul as they are for us. Can we, with the Pharisees, hope that the good things we do will cover over the evil in our hearts? No, according to Jesus, that is the wrong answer. *There is in fact nothing I can do to save myself.*

But thankfully, that's not the end of the story. There is a right answer to God's question, "Why should I let you into heaven?" According to the Bible, the right answer has to do with God's *grace*.

The right answer is something like this: "God, you should let me into heaven, not because of anything I've done, but because of what Christ has done." In other words, it's not about the good things *we've* done for God, but rather it's about the good thing *Christ* has done for us. He died on the cross so that we could be forgiven our sin. He was abandoned so that we could be accepted.

Please turn with me to Ephesians chapter 2, verses 8 and 9:

➤ *Read aloud Ephesians 2:8–9.*

So we are saved by *faith*, by placing our trust in what Jesus did for us on the cross. We're not saved by anything we do, by being nice people, by paying our bills on time, or by going to church or reading the Bible. No, we are saved from eternal punishment by Jesus' death on the cross, and it's a gift. You can't earn it "by works." You can't boast about it. "It is the gift of God."

The only forgiveness available to us is the forgiveness earned by what *Christ* did. Because only Christ's death deals with the problem of the human heart.

Les Misérables[3] tells the story of a criminal, Jean Valjean. A tough, bitter man, he has spent nineteen years in prison. When he is finally released, he finds it impossible to find work or shelter because no-one wants anything to do with him. But finally he

---

[3] Victor Hugo, *Les Misérables* (trans. Norman Denny; London: Penguin, 1982), quotations from pp. 110–11

is taken in by a kindly bishop, who gives him food and a place to stay. However, in the middle of the night, Valjean creeps downstairs and steals the bishop's silver. He is quickly caught by three constables and brought back to the bishop's house.

Things look desperate for Valjean. The bishop has the opportunity to incriminate him for his act of betrayal and have him imprisoned for the rest of his life. But instead, the bishop says this: "So here you are! I'm delighted to see you. Had you forgotten that I gave you the candlesticks as well? They're silver like the rest, and worth a good 200 francs. Did you forget to take them?" So the constables let Valjean go.

After they've gone, the bishop insists that he keep the silver *and the candlesticks*, and tells him: "Do not forget, do not ever forget that you have promised me to use the money to make yourself an honest man." So a stunned Valjean is released and given the silver candlesticks as well. Valjean stutters, "Why? Why are you doing this?" The bishop replies, "Jean Valjean, my brother, you no longer belong to evil. With this silver I have bought your soul and now I am giving you back to God."

Now the bishop could have treated Valjean in one of three ways.

Firstly, he could have treated Valjean with *justice*. Given him exactly what his deeds deserved. He could have said, "Give me back my silver," got the constables to arrest him, and have him packed off back to prison. That would be justice, simply giving him what he deserves – no more, no less.

Alternatively, he could have treated Valjean with *leniency*. He could have said, "I want my silver back, but I won't press charges." That would be leniency – giving him a little bit less than he deserves.

The last option open to the bishop is the option he actually takes: he treats Valjean with *grace*. He says, "I know what you've done, how you've abused my generosity, but look, keep the silver and take these candlesticks as well. You can go free. The only thing I ask is that you use the money to change your life for the better." He gives the criminal standing before him a very expensive gift – one that is totally undeserved. That is grace, treating him with undeserved love and generosity.

We will never understand Christianity until we see ourselves in exactly the same position as Valjean. All of us stand before God as Valjean stood before the bishop: utterly guilty, deserving judgement for the way we've abused his love for us, and with no way of putting the situation right.

CHRISTIANITY
E✝PLORED

But rather than treating us as we deserve, God in his amazing grace and generosity offers us forgiveness – forgiveness that is made possible by Jesus' death on the cross. And remember that this forgiveness is "the gift of God." There's nothing I can do to earn it.

The right answer, again, is: "I trust in what Jesus did for me on the cross: *that's* why I should be allowed into heaven." Of course, we can only give that answer when we realize that we are powerless to save ourselves. We turn to God in utter dependence and weakness, realizing that nothing *we do* will be enough to cure the problem of the human heart.

Not surprisingly, some people find this very hard. It is difficult not only to admit how weak and dependent they are, but also to accept that anything so costly could be given to them for free. It is hard to accept this gift from God when all our lives we've been taught that we have to earn our supper, earn our praise, earn our salary. But the truth is that the Christian life is not about duty. It's about receiving a gift I don't deserve, and then living a life of thanks for that gift. In fact *"charis,"* the Greek word for grace, also means "rejoice."

And we know that as soon as we accept that gift, we will have eternal life in heaven. We are accepted by God. But what happens in the meantime?

Victor Hugo wrote, "Life's greatest happiness is to be convinced we are loved."[4] And in *Les Misérables* we see that the grace that Valjean receives from the bishop changes his life. It unlocks his heart and unleashes his potential. He is ransomed from fear and hatred and becomes a human being of remarkable generosity and mercy, touching numerous lives. It all stems from the new identity he found when the bishop treated him with grace.

You see, God's grace allows me to find my identity, my ultimate worth as a human being, because God knows exactly what I'm like, and yet he loves me anyway. And that is such a relief! Grace means God knows all about my sin and yet he loves me unconditionally. The cross makes that very clear, because even though he knows what I'm like, Christ still died on my behalf. The very person who will ultimately judge the world loves me completely and unalterably. What greater proof of love could there be than to die for someone? Although we are more sinful than we ever realized, we are more loved than we ever dreamed.

---

[4] Victor Hugo, *Les Misérables* (trans. Norman Denny; London: Penguin, 1982).

This unconditional love means three things:

➤ *Display the following headings and read them aloud.*

> **There are no masks to wear**
>
> **There is nothing to prove**
>
> **There are no grudges to bear**

THERE ARE NO MASKS TO WEAR

Firstly, there are no masks to wear. As Philip Yancey says in his book *What's So Amazing About Grace?*, there is "nothing I can do to make God love me more, and there is nothing I can do to make him love me less."[5] God knows exactly what I'm like, and yet he still loves me. *That means I don't have to pretend with God.* There's no hiding behind masks.

Have you ever been worried that your friends would think badly of you for something? Perhaps you've been concerned about being misunderstood or about your reputation being harmed, so you've kept things quiet. But God knows the absolute truth about us – and it's much worse than our friends think. God knows the truth, and yet he still loves me. So I don't have to wear a mask because I'm loved unconditionally. It's an extraordinary relief to no longer have to hide the truth about ourselves.

THERE IS NOTHING TO PROVE

Second, there is nothing to prove. The diver Greg Louganis was once asked how he performed so well under pressure. He replied: "Even if I blow this dive, my mother will still love me."[6] You see, he reminds himself of the one relationship that will remain the same, whatever his performance. Louganis has nothing to prove to his mother. She loves him anyway.

---

[5] Philip Yancey, *What's So Amazing About Grace?* (Grand Rapids: Zondervan, 1997), p. 71.
[6] Greg Louganis, Olympic gold medallist, taken from an interview at the Pan American Games.

CHRISTIANITY
E✝PLORED

And in the same way, if you've put your trust in Christ, you've got nothing to prove to God. Now, that is a great truth because we live in a culture of conditional love. At school, we're told over and over again, "If you get the right grades, we'll affirm you and make you feel loved. But if you don't, we'll withdraw that love." As we get older, love always seems to come with a price tag: "I'll love you if you are young enough, successful enough, beautiful enough, talented enough, thin enough..." and so it goes on. People's whole lives can be conditioned by the sense that, unless they constantly prove themselves, they won't be loved.

But the Christian life isn't like that. The Christian life is motivated not by conditional love, but by unconditional love. It's not about duty or proving yourself. It's about receiving a gift you don't deserve and can't earn, and then living a life of thanks for that gift.

THERE ARE NO GRUDGES TO BEAR

Third, there are no grudges to bear. You see, God's grace effects every other relationship we have. Jesus taught his followers to pray, "Forgive us our sins, for we also forgive everyone who sins against us."[7] Now, as you know, forgiving people who wrong you is an extremely difficult thing to do! But it's so much easier to forgive others when we remember how much God has forgiven us in the first place.

So this is grace: God sending Christ to die on the cross so that I can be forgiven, even though I've done nothing to earn it, even though I deserve punishment. In the light of that, there is no need to pretend we're something we're not or boast about what we've achieved, and there is every reason to freely forgive those who wrong us.

I hope you can see that although you are more sinful than you ever realized, you are more loved than you ever dreamed.

---

[7] Luke 11:4.

AT THE END OF THE TALK

Let me leave you with the following questions for your groups:

➤ *Display the following questions and read them aloud.*

- **If you were in the bishop's place, would you have given Valjean the candlesticks as well?**

- **Has grace made a difference to your view of God?**

- **What do people generally do to be accepted by God, if they bother at all?**

➤ *Allow 30 minutes for groups to work together through the* Study Guide *section called GROUP DISCUSSION 2.*

AT THE END OF THE DISCUSSION

Before next time, use the HOME STUDY section in your *Study Guide* to help you as you continue to read through Mark.

➤ *Remind participants about the weekend or day away, and hand out invitations and schedules.*

CHRISTIANITY
E✝PLORED

JESUS
- HIS RESURRECTION

BEFORE THE TALK

➤ *Welcome the course participants and suggest they take 20 minutes to work through the* Study Guide *section called GROUP DISCUSSION 1 with their group.*

THE TALK

➤ *Deliver the talk. The wording below is intended only as a general guide. The aim of the talk is to present the facts of Christ's resurrection and to show how they bring both hope and a warning.*

Last week we saw that forgiveness is a gift, paid for by Jesus Christ. We don't deserve it, and we can't earn it. And that is grace: God behaving towards us in a way we simply don't deserve. Remember the line in Ephesians: "For it is by grace you have been saved, through faith – and this not from yourselves, it is the gift of God – not by works, so that no one can boast." So in other words, it's faith in what Jesus has done that saves us. Nothing else.

We've seen that Christ's death brings us forgiveness. This week, we'll see what his resurrection adds to that.

All of us know we're going to die – the only uncertainty is exactly when. We are mortal, and each one of us will die. We all have a terminal disease, it's called "life," and its fatality rate is 100%. The question I have for you is this: How do you cope with the certainty of death? And not just the certainty of your *own* death, but also the deaths of those people you love.

Ministers have some thankless tasks. And one of them is standing at the graveside, throwing some soil into the grave, and saying these words from Psalm 103: "As for man, his days are like grass, he flourishes like a flower of the field; the wind blows over it and it is gone, and its place remembers it no more." But that's the truth. Our lives are brief, and however flourishing they have been, they soon come to an end. This is a miserable start to the evening, isn't it?

Now, Jesus was in his early thirties when he died. And yet here we are, two thousand years later, still discussing his life. You see, if Jesus had not apparently risen from the dead, we would probably never even have heard of him. But his resurrection changes everything.

At the end of his account of Jesus' death, Mark focuses on three women who have watched the whole gruesome ordeal. Please turn with me to Mark 15, and we'll start to read from verse 40.

➤ *Read aloud Mark 15:40 – 16:3.*

➤ *You will need to have the following headings ready for display, gradually revealing each of the headings as the talk progresses.*

The shadow of death

The shock of discovery

The significance for the disciples

THE SHADOW OF DEATH

So point 1 – the shadow of death. It was unusual for crucifixion to result in death so quickly, so in verse 44 the Roman governor Pontius Pilate queries the centurion – the same centurion who had stood only a short distance from the cross and watched the extraordinary way in which Jesus had died. The centurion confirms that yes, Jesus had indeed already died. The Romans had many talents, but when it came to killing people, they were experts. So the centurion's words would have been confirmation enough. Having established that Jesus is dead, Pilate gives Joseph permission to remove the body from the cross.

Not only have the women watched Jesus die, but two of them also watch him being buried. Verse 47 says: "Mary Magdalene and Mary the mother of Joses saw where he was laid." They, too, are witnesses of his death.

Now we come to Mark chapter 16, verses 1–3, about thirty-six hours later. The women return to the tomb that they had watched Jesus being buried in. They don't go hoping that Jesus might be alive; they go expecting to find a corpse. Things could not be more dismal – they are grieving and afraid because the young man they've loved and served has been murdered. Jesus' other followers are still in hiding. They don't even think they will be able to get to his body, because they know that a huge stone has been laid across the entrance to the tomb. And that brings us to our second point: the shock of discovery.

THE SHOCK OF DISCOVERY

Let's continue reading from Mark 16, verse 4. In this passage, the women are subjected to three shocks of escalating intensity.

➤ *Read aloud Mark 16:4–8.*

The first shock comes in verse 4: "But when they looked up, they saw that the stone, which was very large, had been rolled away." In the original Greek, this phrase literally means "hurled out." There is no need for them to worry about the stone because divine power has dealt with it.

Then comes the second shock as they go inside the tomb. Look again at verse 5: "As they entered the tomb, they saw a young man dressed in a white robe sitting on the right side, and they were alarmed." They see a man whose appearance is so striking that it causes the Roman soldiers guarding the tomb to shake. Matthew tells us that they become "like dead men."[1] The women, understandably, are terrified. But they are not delusional – the man affirms the reality of what is happening in verse 6: "Don't be alarmed," he said. "You are looking for Jesus the Nazarene, who was crucified." Yes, the man from Nazareth, the one you've been following these past three years, was killed. "See the place where they laid him." He was really buried here; you don't have the wrong address. The fact is that Jesus simply isn't here anymore.

---

[1] Matthew 28:4.

But the third shock will change the women's lives forever. It comes as the young man in the empty tomb tells them the reason why Jesus' body is not there. Verse 6: "He has risen!" Just as there was no need for them to be worried about the stone, there is now no need for the spices they'd brought to anoint the corpse. Divine power has not only flung the stone away – it has also raised a body to life. This is supernatural. The tomb was empty because Jesus isn't dead anymore. He is alive.

So how do the women react to this staggering news? Verse 8 says: "Trembling and bewildered, the women went out and fled from the tomb. They said nothing to anyone, because they were afraid."

Why are they afraid? Because they've forgotten what Jesus told them would happen. Look at the young man's words in verse 7: "...go, tell his disciples and Peter, 'He is going ahead of you into Galilee. There you will see him, *just as he told you.*'" Jesus had told them repeatedly that he would suffer, die and rise again. Mark chapter 8: "The Son of Man must be killed and after three days rise again." Mark chapter 9: "They will kill him and after three days he will rise." Mark chapter 10: "The Gentiles will mock him and spit on him, flog him and kill him. Three days later he will rise."

Jesus is always in control. He knows exactly how he will die, what will happen to him beyond death, and he explains everything to them before it happens. By now, the women should have learned to take Jesus at his word. And so should we.

That leads us to our third heading: the significance for the disciples.

THE SIGNIFICANCE FOR THE DISCIPLES

The young man said that the disciples would see Jesus in Galilee. And that is precisely what happens. The disciples do see him and finally believe that Jesus had indeed risen from the dead. Well, most of them believe. All except one, in fact.

John records a wonderful incident in his Gospel. Please turn to John chapter 20, verse 24. Here we read about one of the disciples – a man called Thomas – who refuses to believe that Jesus has risen. The other disciples tell Thomas that they've seen Jesus. But Thomas knows that once people die, they don't come back. He insists not only on seeing Jesus for himself, but also on touching him, as if to prove that this vision is not some kind of ghost or communal hallucination.

CHRISTIANITY
E✝PLORED

➤ *Read aloud John 20:24–25.*

So Thomas says, "Unless I touch his open wounds, I'm not going to believe it." And of course he wouldn't offer to go poking around in someone else's open wounds unless he was certain that it wasn't going to happen. Let's read on from verse 26.

➤ *Read aloud John 20:26–28.*

What can Thomas say? The proof of the resurrection is standing right in front of him. Well, he says this: "My Lord and my God!" Thirty years later, this stubborn, rational, incredulous man was to die a martyr's death testifying to what he had seen.

The resurrection turned a group of disciples cowering in fear for their lives into preachers of awesome courage.

The Gospels alone tell us of eleven separate instances where Jesus is seen after his death, at different times and in different places, to different people. In 1 Corinthians chapter 15, Paul tells us that over five hundred people saw Jesus at one time, many of whom were still living when Paul was writing. So Paul was saying to his readers, "If you don't believe me, go and talk to the eyewitnesses. They're still alive and will confirm the truth of what I'm saying."

So if the resurrection actually happened, what conclusions can we draw?

➤ *Display the following headings.*

The resurrection means:

a great hope

a great warning

A GREAT HOPE

The first conclusion is that the resurrection gives us great hope. Why? Because it means we can confidently put our trust in the person who said this: "I am the resurrection and the life. He who believes in me will live, even though he dies; and whoever lives and believes in me will never die."[2] The resurrection conclusively demonstrates Jesus' power and authority over death – not just over his own, but also over ours.

---

2 John 11:25–26.

The first funeral of a young person I ever conducted was that of a professional musician called Stuart Spencer, who died of cancer in his thirties. He was a deeply committed Christian, and we became close friends. I will always remember my last visit to him. It was three days before he died. I was feeling emotional and suddenly just blurted out what was on my mind. It was out before I knew it. I just said, "Stuart, what's it like to die?" And I will never forget his answer. He said very calmly, "Rico, Christ has risen. He is risen." Stuart knew Christ had risen, and so he knew what he had to look forward to beyond death.

1 Thessalonians chapter 4, verse 14 explains that just as Christ died and rose again, so Christians, when they die, will rise again: "We believe that Jesus died and rose again and so we believe that God will bring with Jesus those who have fallen asleep in him."

Revelation, the last book of the Bible, gives us a privileged glimpse of what heaven will be like. Look at Revelation 21, verses 3 and 4.

➤ *Read aloud Revelation 21:3–4.*

Think of the most mind-blowing experience you've ever had, the most intimate relationship you've ever shared, the deepest enchantment, the most euphoric joy. Well, multiply that moment's intensity by infinity and its duration by eternity; then you are close to what it will feel like being with Christ in heaven. "There will be *no more death or mourning or crying or pain.*" In other words, we won't have to put up with sin any more. At last, we will be free to enjoy all of the good things that God provides, eternally. As it says in Revelation, God himself will wipe every tear from our eyes. There will be no more regret, no more unfulfilled dreams, no more lost loved ones, no more fear, no more bitterness, no more broken hearts, no more loneliness, no more sin. And the Bible affirms that heaven is not a place where individuality is lost. Far from it. It's a physical place – as real as the one we're in now – where all our potential as individuals is finally fulfilled. This is not a pipe dream, or a cruel mirage, but an amazing reality earned for us by Christ's death, and proved by Christ's resurrection.

However, although the resurrection is a great hope for those who follow Christ, it is also a great warning for those who ignore him.

CHRISTIANITY
EXPLORED

As we saw in the parable of the tenants that we looked at earlier in our GROUP DISCUSSION, a time will come when we will be judged. The resurrection is proof of that: just as death was not the end for Jesus, so it won't be the end for us. Please turn to Acts chapter 17, verse 31.

➤ *Read aloud Acts 17:31.*

At first the thought of a day of reckoning may appear very distressing – especially if, like me, you don't just fear for yourself but also for loved ones. But actually it's a very good thing indeed, and the alternative to judgement is absolutely appalling.

The book *Schindler's List* tells of an incident in Krakow, in Poland, during World War II, when the SS guards are moving Jews from their ghetto in the town to a concentration camp outside. Oscar Schindler, the hero of the story, sees a mother and son brutally murdered by the guards. What shocks him most is that it all happened in full view of a young girl, about three years old, who stood out because she was dressed in red. The author writes, "Later in the day after he had absorbed a ration of brandy, Oscar understood the proposition in its clearest terms: they permitted witnesses, such witnesses as the red toddler, because they believed all the witnesses would perish too."[3] Do you see the implication of that? The Nazi guards did what they liked because they thought they would never have to give an account of their actions. As far as the guards were concerned, there would be no day of reckoning, no accounting for what they'd done, no judgement. They could do whatever they liked and nothing mattered. Because all those with the power to condemn them would be dead.

But death is not the end, as we've seen. Thankfully, the Bible repeatedly assures us that wrongdoing will not be left unaddressed – ultimately there will be justice. The Bible is very blunt and clear about this. The book of Hebrews, for example, says this: "man is destined to die once, and after that to face judgement."[4]

It's a sobering thought, but the alternative is much more terrifying. Do any of us really want to live in a world where nothing matters, where even the most extreme cruelty is met with vacuous silence? But justice *will* be done, every sin *will* be paid for – that is the promise of the resurrection. There *is* a place called hell – it is a place of isolation, punishment and torment. It is a place where we pay for our sin ourselves.

---

[3] Thomas Keneally, *Schindler's List* (London: Sceptre, 1994), p. 143.
[4] Hebrews 9:27.

Paul preached that message to the people of Athens. He told them that, ultimately, God will judge everyone, and that he "has given proof of this to all men by raising [Jesus] from the dead." Obviously, no-one likes being told about judgement, so how do these people react? Look at Acts 17, verse 32.

➤ *Read aloud Acts 17:32–34.*

So some of them sneered, and some wanted to hear more on the subject. We also read that some believed. What's your reaction to the resurrection?

"For [God] has set a day when he will judge the world with justice by the man he has appointed." And who is this "appointed" man? The resurrection confirms the answer. It is God's only Son, a man who knows all about Thomas' doubts before he even speaks, a man who knows all about us and yet still gave up his life for us.

AT THE END OF THE TALK

Let me leave you with the following questions for your groups:

➤ *Display the following questions and read them aloud.*

- **"Heaven is not a pipe dream, or a cruel mirage, but an amazing reality earned for us by Christ's death, and proved by Christ's resurrection." Has this changed your view of heaven?**

- **"For God has set a day when he will judge the world with justice by the man he has appointed. He has given proof of this to all men by raising him from the dead" (Acts 17:31). What's your reaction to this?**

- **Do you believe the resurrection is possible?**

➤ *Allow 30 minutes for groups to work together through the* Study Guide *section called GROUP DISCUSSION 2.*

AT THE END OF THE DISCUSSION

Before next time, use the HOME STUDY section in your *Study Guide* to help you as you continue to read through Mark. Once you've done that, you will have read through the whole of Mark's Gospel.

➤ *Remind participants about the weekend or day away, and hand out invitations and schedules.*

CHRISTIANITY
E✝PLORED

EXPLORING CHRISTIAN LIFE

THE CHURCH

BEFORE THE TALK

➤ *Welcome the course participants – the wording below is intended only as a general guide.*

Welcome to the weekend / day away. I'm so pleased you've made time to do this.

➤ *If you have arranged for someone to begin this session by sharing his or her testimony, introduce that person at this point. Ideally, their testimony should last no more than 3 minutes.*

There was an old man who made his living by organizing dogfights. He had two dogs, a white one and a black one. Every Saturday he would let them fight each other and he'd take bets on who would win. Some weeks the black dog would win, and other weeks the white dog would win. But the old man always guessed right. His friends began to ask him how he did it, and eventually he admitted: "During the week I starve one and feed the other. The one I feed always wins because he is stronger."

Now, the Bible tells us that there are two natures struggling for mastery within us: the spiritual nature and the sinful nature. So which one will dominate us? The spiritual nature or the sinful nature? It depends on which one we feed.

And that's why it's so important to understand the role of the church, the Holy Spirit, prayer and the Bible in the Christian life. All these things work together to feed our spiritual lives. We'll be looking at all four of these during our time together, and I'd like us to start by exploring the role of the church.

> *Deliver the talk. The wording below is intended only as a general guide. The aim of the talk is to explain why the support of other Christians is vital in the Christian life.*

When the Bible talks about "the church," it's not referring to a building or old-fashioned institution. It's simply talking about all those who have put their trust in Christ. And God wants these people, this "church," to be a support to one another.

In Hebrews chapter 10, verse 25, we read this: "Let us not give up meeting together, as some are in the habit of doing, but let us encourage one another." The writer knows that, without this mutual encouragement, it will be hard to persevere in the Christian life. Very hard indeed. Because we often feel that we're on our own.

That's the background for a letter that Peter wrote. It's called 1 Peter and you can find it on page ..... of your Bible. So let's start by looking at what Peter says about the Christian life.

> *Read aloud 1 Peter 1:1–7.*

Peter wrote this letter from Rome, in the early sixties AD, when the emperor was a young man called Nero. Now, I don't know what you were up to on *your* seventeenth birthday, but in AD 54, Nero became ruler of the world: the head of the most powerful empire on the planet, the Roman Empire. This wasn't an ideal state of affairs. At seventeen, you can be a bit impetuous. And whereas most of us were probably in school, or stacking shelves on a Saturday morning, Nero was indulging his lust for power by murdering everyone he thought was against him. As Nero's reign continued, his venom increasingly turned against Christians.

In AD 64, a fire destroyed half the city of Rome and word got around that Nero was responsible because he wanted Rome cleared to make room for a massive building project. Nero, sensing that public opinion was turning against him, passed the blame onto the Christians. He claimed that they had brought a curse on the city because they wouldn't worship the Roman gods. As a result, people who insisted on their allegiance to Christ were arrested, imprisoned and executed, often by being thrown to wild animals.[1] Indeed Peter, who wrote this letter, would one day be martyred – crucified upside down because he refused to die as Christ did.

---

[1] See Tacitus, *Annals 15.44*, taken from *The History of Christianity* (Oxford: Lion Publishing, 1990).

So that is the context of this letter. Peter wrote it as the Roman Empire became more and more violently opposed to the Christian faith. And the Christians Peter is writing to here were those who had fled from the persecution in Rome and Jerusalem. So ironically the message of Christ, the good news of the gospel, was actually spreading throughout the Roman world because of persecution. And the places the Christians had fled to were now following Nero's lead and becoming increasingly hostile.

So, in verse 1, Peter addresses himself to: "God's elect, strangers in the world, scattered throughout Pontus, Galatia, Cappadocia, Asia and Bithynia..."

These Christians are "strangers in the world" because they find themselves surrounded by people who have no idea why they believe what they do. And the same is true of Christians today. If you decide to follow Jesus, there is a degree to which you do become a stranger in the world. In the office, the word can go around that you've gone religious, and – if you stand up for Christ – you can find yourself politely frozen out. You could even lose your job. You can also find the same thing happening in your family. They may not understand what has happened to you. They may start asking, "Wasn't our upbringing good enough for you?" Friends may decide that they don't want to spend time with you anymore, because they feel awkward around you. It can be terribly hard being a stranger in the world.

➤ At this point, you might want to ask one of the leaders to give a testimony illustrating what it means to be a "stranger in the world."

So why not just blend into the background? Isn't it better not to be too enthusiastic and committed rather than be misunderstood, rejected and frozen out?

Peter's letter addresses this issue head-on. Whatever the pressure, remember *who you are*. Look at verses 1 and 2 again: "To God's elect... who have been *chosen* according to the foreknowledge of God the Father..." So who are you? You are God's elect, God's chosen people. These verses remind us that we become followers of Jesus not just because we make a choice. We become followers of Jesus because *God* chooses *us*. So when you are rejected by people, and that can be so painful, remember that you've been chosen by God.

And remember *what you have* because God has chosen you. Look at verses 3 and 4.

➤ Read aloud 1 Peter 1:3–4.

Because God has chosen you, you have a living hope. You can be certain about your future because of Jesus Christ's resurrection from the dead. He got through death himself so he can get you through death and give you eternal life. And this is an inheritance that can never perish, spoil or fade.

The problem with the life we're living now is that *everything* perishes, spoils or fades. You buy a new car and it rusts, you're excited about your promotion at work and the excitement fades, you buy a new shirt, spill something on it, and that's it – it's spoiled. We can choose to invest in the things of this world, which perish, spoil and fade. Or we can invest in the things of the next world, which don't.

This future with Christ in heaven is not something that you can lose, and it's not temporary like the life we're living now. No, this inheritance is certain and eternal. God has chosen you and given you that certain future. And look at the next verse: "In this you greatly rejoice, though now for a little while you may have had to suffer grief in all kinds of trials."

Now let me stop here and make one thing clear – if it isn't already – 99.9% of the blessings of the Christian life are in the world to come. And if you think that sounds like an exaggeration, see if you still feel the same way in a thousand years. Or ten thousand years. Don't get me wrong, I love being a Christian now; it's a life of such purpose. It is a great joy to know Christ and his forgiveness. But nevertheless, 99.9% of the blessings in the Christian life are in the world to come.

The Christian life is full of trials, but one way of persevering through them – and even rejoicing – is to remember the inheritance that God himself has provided for you. And it is vital to remind ourselves of all these truths by spending time with the church, with those who understand and share your trust in Jesus.

Peter tells us how we should treat those in the church. Look at verse 22.

➤ *Read aloud 1 Peter 1:22.*

Peter says that this love must be "sincere." Literally, the word means "not hypocritical." And the word "deeply" in the Greek means "strenuously." It's not to be pretended; it is to be something genuine.

CHRISTIANITY
E╳PLORED

Peter is commanding Christians to "love one another deeply." He's not talking here about human affection. He's not talking about loving because we find another person lovable or attractive or because they love us in return. No, this sort of love is being commanded because the church is the Christian's family. He's saying that because God is your "Father," other Christians are your brothers and sisters, so you must love them. And, of course, it works both ways. It's tremendous to be loved and supported by other Christians.

Here is a quote written by a non-Christian in AD 125 about the Christian community: "...they walk in all humility and kindness, and falsehood is not found among them, and they love one another: ...and he who has gives to him who has not, without grudging; and when they see a stranger they bring him to their dwellings, and rejoice over him as over a true brother; for they do not call brothers those who are after the flesh, but those who are in the spirit and in God."[2]

Proverbs chapter 13, verse 20 says this: "He who walks with the wise grows wise, but a companion of fools suffers harm."

We are deeply affected by our friends. I don't suppose that comes as a surprise to you, but it is an easy truth to forget. The values, convictions and morals of the people you walk closely with will find their way into your own life. So, if you're walking with people whose judgements are faulty, then they'll cause you to suffer harm.

So if you're a Christian, it's very important to find a church where the teaching is faithful to God's word, where the people you meet welcome and support you, and where you are able to serve others. Sadly, not every church you visit will do these things. So don't be afraid to keep looking until you find one that does.

Whatever you do, don't go through life walking alone.

---

[2] *The Apology of Aristides.* According to Eusebius, Aristides delivered the *Apology* when Hadrian visited Athens in AD 125. The text was discovered in the Convent of St. Catherine on Mount Sinai in the nineteenth century. Taken from Helen B. Harris, *The Newly Recovered Apology of Aristides: Its Doctrines and Ethics* (London: Hodder & Stoughton, 1891), pp. 106–107.

Let me leave you with the following questions for your groups:

➤ *Display the following questions and read them aloud.*

- **"He who walks with the wise grows wise, but a companion of fools suffers harm" (Proverbs 13:20). Do you think this is true in your own experience?**

- **"...love one another deeply, from the heart" (1 Peter 1:22). Do you think this is realistic?**

➤ *Allow 30 minutes for groups to work together through the* Study Guide *section called GROUP DISCUSSION.*

CHRISTIANITY
EXPLORED

BEFORE THE TALK

➤ *If you have arranged for someone to begin this session by sharing his or her testimony, introduce that person at this point. Ideally, their testimony should last no more than 3 minutes.*

➤ *Give a brief introduction – the wording below is intended only as a general guide.*

We now move on to another reason why we're not alone in the Christian life: the Holy Spirit. The Bible shows very clearly that there is only one God, and yet there are three personal distinctions in his nature. I'm sure you've heard people referring to them: God the Father, God the Son, and God the Holy Spirit. I'd like us now to look in more detail at the Holy Spirit.

> *Deliver the talk. The wording below is intended only as a general guide. The aim of the talk is to show how the Holy Spirit works in a person's life, both before and after the person becomes a Christian. The talk opens by explaining who the Holy Spirit is, then goes on to explore aspects of his work: he convicts people of their sin, provides "gifts," gives people the desire to obey God, fights against the sinful nature and brings peace.*

There was once a photographer who was taking photos of a raging Australian bush fire. Eventually the fire became too intense for him, so he radioed for a small plane to pick him up and take him over the fire. He was assured that there would be a plane waiting for him at a nearby airstrip, and so he hurried around to the airfield. Sure enough, there on the runway was a small plane exactly as he had been told. He jumped in and said to the pilot, "Take her away." When they were in the air he said to the pilot, "I want you to swing left and go low over the fire." A little later he said, "Now I want you to dive down onto the top of the smoke." The pilot turned to him and said, "Why are you asking me to do this?" And the photographer replied, "Because I'm a photographer and I want good photos." To which the pilot exclaimed, "You mean you're not my instructor?"

Now thankfully, if you become a Christian, you'll be joined by an expert instructor: the Holy Spirit.

Turn with me to John chapter 14, verse 23.

> *Read aloud John 14:23.*

If you become a Christian, Jesus promises in this verse that he and his Father will come and make their home with you. How exactly can this happen?

Look at what Jesus says a few verses earlier in John 14, verse 15.

> *Read aloud John 14:15–17.*

Jesus explains that the "Counsellor" will come to live "in" those who obey him. Who is this "Counsellor"? Well, look at verse 26. The "Counsellor" is "the Holy Spirit." So, in other words, the Father and the Son make their home with us through the Holy Spirit. It's a miraculous thing that happens to those who put their trust in Jesus: the Holy Spirit will come to live "with you" and "in you."

Notice, too, that Jesus talks in verse 16 about "*another* Counsellor." In effect, he is saying that this Spirit will do for believers what he himself has done for them while on earth: teach them, guide them and enable them to understand God's word. Indeed, the Spirit who comes to live in Christians is the Spirit of Christ himself. It's as if Jesus is actually with us.

The Greek word Jesus uses for "Counsellor" is "*parakletos,*" which comes from two words, "*para,*" meaning "alongside," and "*kaleo,*" meaning "to call." So this "Counsellor" is literally "the one who is called alongside." The Greeks used the word "*parakletos*" to describe a friend comforting a bereaved person or a pilot taking a ship into port. So the Holy Spirit is someone who comes to comfort and guide.

Jesus talks about the "Counsellor" again in John 16. Let's start reading from verse 7.

➤ *Read aloud John 16:7–8.*

The key word here is the verb "convict." It is a word taken from the law courts and used in the Greek-speaking world to describe the cross-examination of a witness. Jesus tells us here that he will send the Holy Spirit to cross-examine men and women. So the Spirit makes people aware that they have rejected Jesus, that they are sinful, that they need to be made righteous, that there will be a judgement. He opens our eyes to see our desperate state before God and our need of his forgiveness, made possible for us through Jesus' death.

➤ *At this point, you might want to ask one of the leaders to give a testimony illustrating the way in which the Holy Spirit prompted him or her to become a Christian.*

One of the amazing things about the Holy Spirit is that he gives each of Jesus' followers different gifts. The apostle Paul insists that every Christian has a unique role to play in God's church and that he or she is to fulfill that role according to the "gifts" that the Holy Spirit has given him or her. These gifts can be anything – anything that will help other Christians. In 1 Corinthians chapter 12 we read: "There are different kinds of gifts, but the same Spirit. There are different kinds of service, but the same Lord... Now to each one the manifestation of the Spirit is given for the common good." Now, these gifts are to be used "for the common good." They're not there to make us feel important as individuals. They're given to us so that we can benefit one another.

That obviously prompts the question, "So what are my gifts?" The New Testament lists the gifts of the Spirit in four passages: Romans chapter 12, verses 6–8; 1 Corinthians chapter 12, verses 8–10; Ephesians chapter 4, verse 11 and 1 Peter chapter 4, verses 10–11. You can look these up in your group during the discussion if you like.

Turn with me now to Ezekiel chapter 36, and we'll read verses 26–27. Here God explains what will happen when he gives Christians his Spirit.

➤ *Read aloud Ezekiel 36:26–27.*

The Spirit will change Christians' hearts, giving them the desire to obey laws that would otherwise seem too hard to obey. As the apostle Paul says in Romans chapter 7, verse 22: "In my inner being I delight in God's law." That longing in your heart to go God's way is a sign that the Holy Spirit is at work in your life.

Although the Holy Spirit makes us delight in God's law, the presence of the Spirit is not always a comfortable experience, because he is constantly at war with our sinful nature. In the Bayeux Tapestry[1] there is a picture of a Norman soldier running out of the battle, scared stiff. The next picture shows a bishop prodding him in the rear to get him back in the fight, and the caption says, "The bishop comforts his soldier." That's a good picture of the Holy Spirit. Sometimes he prods Christians to live a life more worthy of Christ.

The apostle Paul writes this in Galatians chapter 5: "the sinful nature desires what is contrary to the Spirit, and the Spirit what is contrary to the sinful nature." Just as Jesus convicted people of the sin in their lives, so his Spirit does the same. For example, Jesus frequently accused the Pharisees of hypocrisy. In the same way, the Spirit accuses us when we call ourselves Christians but fail to live in the way we should.

But this battle between the Spirit and the sinful nature is also something to be thankful for, because it confirms that Christ's Spirit is within you, sensitizing your conscience, giving you a longing to be more like him, fighting against everything that keeps you from knowing God more fully. But I promise you this: this battle between the sinful nature and the Spirit will continue until the day you die.

---

[1] Craftsman unknown, "Bayeux Tapestry," Museum of Queen Matilda, Bayeux, France (11th century).

Boris Becker, the German tennis player, once said, "I'd won Wimbledon twice before, once as the youngest player. I was rich: I had all the material possessions I could want – money, cars, women – everything. I know this is a cliché. It's the old song of the movie and pop star who committed suicide; they had everything yet they are so unhappy. I had no inner peace." You see, Boris Becker could have everything the world has to offer, but if he doesn't have a relationship with the God who made him, he will have no peace.

But when a person begins to follow Christ, he or she no longer feels that separation. Indeed, because the Spirit now resides in that person, God has made his home with them forever. His presence provides peace, described in Philippians chapter 4 as "the peace of God, which transcends all understanding." Paul writes in Romans chapter 8 that this peace comes from a deep inner conviction that the follower of Christ is one of "God's children," no longer separated from him, and certain to be with him in heaven. It's the peace that can only come from finding rest in our relationship with our heavenly Father.

Let me leave you with the following questions for your groups:

➤ *Display the following questions and read them aloud.*

• **"I had no inner peace." What is it that makes people feel like this?**

• **Having explored Jesus' life, how would you feel about his Spirit coming to live "with you" and "in you" (John 14:17)?**

➤ *Allow 30 minutes for groups to work together through the* Study Guide *section called GROUP DISCUSSION.*

CHRISTIANITY
E✝PLORED

EXPLORING CHRISTIAN LIFE

PRAYER

BEFORE THE TALK

➤ *If you have arranged for someone to begin this session by sharing his or her testimony, introduce that person at this point. Ideally, their testimony should last no more than 3 minutes.*

➤ *Give a brief introduction – the wording below is intended only as a general guide.*

In this third session, we're going to look at another essential ingredient in the Christian life: prayer.

THE TALK

➤ *Deliver the talk. The wording below is intended only as a general guide. The aim of the talk is to explain why and how Christians pray.*

Most people see prayer as a last resort in a crisis. A crisis comes – be it an exam you are under–prepared for, or a traffic jam when you're late for a meeting – and you think to yourself, "well, there's nothing else I can do, I'd better pray." It's a 999 or 911 call; an emergency service. When nothing else will work, we pray.

Others see prayer as a formula. Perhaps you've been brought up to say your prayers ("God bless Mummy, God bless Daddy and help me to be good") just before you went to bed.

Then there are the sportsmen who can't run onto a field without crossing themselves and saying a little prayer. It becomes a sort of superstition.

Another image of prayer is like this. Picture a deserted little town in a Clint Eastwood western. A monk is standing in front of a dusty church. He is wearing a coarse brown robe with a sort of rope around his waist. His hands are clasped prayerfully together and he looks meek, fragile and undernourished. In front of him is Clint on horseback, with his poncho and his tilted hat. The monk asks, "Let me help you get the bad guys!" Clint replies, "No, it's dangerous and you can't fight." "But I want to help," says the monk, to which Clint contemptuously replies, "Well, I guess you could always pray," as he gallops away to where the action is.

That's certainly many people's view of prayer – it's ineffectual. It's what delicate people do while those who get the job done are out getting the job done.

If that's how you think of prayer, then I have to tell you that the Bible will confront you head-on, because you have failed to understand who Christians pray to.

Please turn to Acts chapter 4, and we will read verses 23–31.

➤ Read aloud Acts 4:23–31.

At this point, the disciples' situation could not get much worse. Their leader has been crucified and their two main spokesmen have just been interrogated by the highest religious authorities, who are determined to shut them up. In the face of this fierce opposition, they pray together. And look at who they pray to in verse 24: the "Sovereign Lord... [who] made the heaven and the earth and the sea, and everything in them."

It's as if they're saying, "Lord, you are sovereign, you made the universe, our world and all the people who live in it, and you're in control of everything, even those people who are threatening us."

Look again at verses 27–28.

➤ Read aloud Acts 4:27–28.

You see, that's who Christians pray to: a God who is unimaginably powerful. However hostile people are towards him, plotting against this "Sovereign Lord" is a complete waste of time. So even though Herod, Pilate, the Gentiles and the people of Israel all conspired to have Jesus killed, "They did what your power and will had decided beforehand should happen."

CHRISTIANITY
E✝PLORED

Their evil plans only succeed in fulfilling what God had already decided should happen. Now, at the time, it must have seemed very different. On the day of the crucifixion, the disciples must have thought that nothing could be worse. But a few months later, they can see that God has always been in control.

That's not to say that God's enemies are puppets who have no choice but to disobey God. The Bible makes it clear that everyone has the choice to obey or to disobey. But the disciples' prayer here gives us a glimpse of just how powerful God is: "They did what your power and will had decided beforehand should happen." You have to be unimaginably powerful to have your enemies do your bidding, even as they seek to destroy you. But that is precisely the kind of God who hears Jesus' followers when they pray.

The disciples – having in mind who God is – then ask for God's help. They pray in verse 29: "Now, Lord, consider their threats and enable your servants to speak your word with great boldness." And God responds to their prayer in a very visible way, as you can see in verse 31: "After they prayed, the place where they were meeting was shaken. And they were all filled with the Holy Spirit and spoke the word of God boldly." By speaking the word of God boldly, they are doing exactly what the authorities have forbidden them to do. You wouldn't do that unless you believed that God was sovereign.

So when you pray it is important to remember who you pray to: the Sovereign Lord, who is in complete control of everything that will happen to you. And of course, if God were not in control, then there would be no point in praying. But, if he is in control, then I can pray about anything.

Talk to people in your group, and they will tell you about the ways God has answered prayer in their lives and in the lives of people they know.

➤ *At this point, you might want to ask one of the leaders to give a testimony illustrating how God has answered prayer in his or her life.*

But that's not all. As well as being "Sovereign Lord," God is also – if you're a Christian – *your Father*.

Please turn to Matthew chapter 6, and we'll read verses 5 and 6.

➤ *Read aloud Matthew 6:5–6.*

It is interesting to ask why the hypocrites in verse 5 stand on the street corners. It's because double the number of people will see them. If you are on the corner people from both streets will see you. "But," Jesus says in 6, "when you pray, go into your room, close the door and pray to your Father."

And look at verse 9.

➤ *Read aloud Matthew 6:9.*

Perhaps the most striking thing here is that Jesus tells his followers to refer to God as "Father." In fact, the word Jesus uses for "Father" is closer to our word "Daddy." There is tremendous intimacy here.

Let me try and illustrate just what a privilege it is to be able to call the Sovereign Lord of the universe "Father." You may remember the picture of President Kennedy working at his desk while his son, John, plays beneath it.[1] Now I think it is safe to say that no other little boy in the world could have got anywhere near that desk, but John could walk straight in and play. Why? Because of his relationship with the President. He would have been able to say to anybody who questioned his presence, "He may be your President, but he's my Daddy." He had a level of access and intimacy that would be impossible for anyone else. It was no small thing for John to be able to play under his father's desk, and it is no small thing for a Christian to call God "Father."

It means that Christians can speak to God as they might speak to a loving earthly father: to thank him, ask him for support or forgiveness, confide in him. Of course, the intimacy Christians have with God is because of the cross. If I try praying to God with my sin still in the way, then my prayers will "bounce off the ceiling," as Isaiah chapter 59, verse 2 says: "your iniquities have separated you from your God; your sins have hidden his face from you, so that he will not hear."

However, because Christ dealt with sin at the cross, Christians are able to talk freely with God. In fact, you may hear Christians end their prayers "in the name of the Lord Jesus." It's a way of acknowledging that Jesus is the one who has given them access to God.

---

[1] Robin Cross, *J.F.K.: A Hidden Life* (London: Bloomsbury, 1992), p. 178.

CHRISTIANITY
E✝PLORED

And, as Christians pray, they develop this relationship with God. Like any relationship, it depends on being yourself – being honest, being natural – and communicating regularly. Psalm 62, verse 8 says this: "Trust in him at all times, O people; pour out your hearts to him, for God is our refuge."

Prayer teaches us to be increasingly dependent on God for all our needs. Now, as you know, dependence on a human being can be a bad thing. But unlike an earthly father, God always has the power to do what is best for those who love him. Nothing is beyond his control or outside his concern. Look with me at what Philippians chapter 4, verse 6 says:

➤ Read aloud Philippians 4:6.

Of course, God doesn't *always* answer prayer in the way we want or expect. We pour out our hearts, but God may not respond in the way we'd like. At moments like this, we have to trust that God is in control, that he has a plan for every single one of us, that he is wiser, more loving and more knowledgeable than we are, and that the decisions he makes are trustworthy. There will be difficult situations that we won't understand until we're with God in heaven.

So when you pray it is important to remember who you pray to. You pray to your Father, the Sovereign Lord who is in complete control of everything that may happen to you. Prayer is not ineffectual. And it's not to be treated only as a last resort in a crisis, or as a superstitious formula.

Spike Milligan was once asked, "Do you ever pray?" and he said, "Yes, I do pray desperately all the time, but I've no idea *who* I'm praying to."[2] For Christians, that's no longer the case.

---

[2] Spike Milligan, author and comedian (1918–2002).

Let me leave you with the following questions for your groups:

➤ *Display the following questions and read them aloud.*

• **Do you ever pray?**

• **God is "the Sovereign Lord, who is in complete control of everything that may happen to you." How might this affect your life?**

➤ *Allow 30 minutes for groups to work together through the* Study Guide *section called GROUP DISCUSSION.*

BEFORE THE TALK

➢ *If you have arranged for someone to begin this session by sharing his or her testimony, introduce that person at this point. Ideally, their testimony should last no more than 3 minutes.*

➢ *Give a brief introduction – the wording below is intended only as a general guide.*

We've seen that the church, the Holy Spirit and prayer are all important sources of support for the Christian. Now lastly we're going to look at the importance of the Bible. Remember that all of these things work together to feed your spiritual life.

> *Deliver the talk. The wording below is intended only as a general guide. The aim of the talk is to emphasize the importance of reading the Bible regularly.*

By way of introduction, let's try answering some simple questions about the Bible: Who wrote it? What's it about? What's it for?

Turn to 2 Timothy chapter 3, and we'll read verses 14–17.

> *Read aloud 2 Timothy 3:14–17.*

So, who actually wrote the Bible? Verse 16 puts it like this: "All Scripture is God-breathed" and 2 Peter chapter 1, verse 21 adds that the Bible "never had its origin in the will of man, but men spoke from God as they were carried along by the Holy Spirit." God decided what would go into the Bible and then he breathed it out, by his Spirit, through the authors.

Question two: What is the Bible about? Well, the Bible contains all kinds of writing. There's history in here, biography, poetry, songs, predictions about the future. But whatever the style, the message is the same. The Bible is about being rescued from what it calls our "sin." It tells us that this sin has broken our relationship with God. It also explains how that relationship can be re-established because of Jesus' death on a cross.

The start of the book, Genesis chapters 1 and 2, tell us that God made the world, entrusted us with everything in it, and intended that we would live in relationship with him. The Bible goes on to explain that, sadly, we turned our backs on him. Wonderfully, however, God doesn't turn his back on us. Ultimately, he sends his Son to die so that we can be forgiven our sin. We read that Jesus overcame death, and the Bible makes it clear that this resurrection ensures eternal life for those who put their trust in him. The Bible also promises that Jesus will return again, next time as judge of the whole world.

On to our last question: what's the Bible for? Well, put simply, it enables us to know God. Please turn with me to Psalm 1.

> *Read aloud Psalm 1.*

Now, this psalm gives us some great advice on how to get to know God.

CHRISTIANITY
E✝PLORED

The first verse is very striking: "Blessed is the man who does not *walk* in the counsel of the *wicked* or *stand* in the way of *sinners* or *sit* in the seat of *mockers*." The psalmist makes it clear that the person who is "blessed" – that is the person of whom God approves – is the person who watches what advice they take, what example they follow and what company they keep. Christians are not to be influenced by the "wicked," "sinners," or "mockers" – those who reject God.

Notice also the three stages of influence: walking with these people; then standing; and finally sitting. Each is more dangerous than the last. The least influential is just walking along listening; a little more influential is standing and discussing in more detail; and most influential of all is actually sitting with these people, taking on board attitudes and ideas.

We're only human, so we want to please those around us. We're influenced by those we spend time with. But the psalm says that the Christian's "delight is in the law of the LORD, and on his law he meditates day and night." So Christians are to take their lead not from the people around them, but from God's law, the Bible. If I want to know how to please God in my marriage, in my family, as a friend or in the workplace, then all the principles I need are here.

➤ *Hold up a Bible.*

And that's not an imposition, that's a joy. Because having seen God's character through Christ, having understood his love for me, I know he wants what is best for me.

Psalm 1 makes it clear that we should be passionate about the Bible, reading it and reflecting upon it continually. The person who does this is described in verse 3 as being "like a tree planted by streams of water, which yields its fruit in season and whose leaf does not wither." Just as the tree draws constant nourishment from the nearby stream, so the Christian is refreshed and replenished by reading the Bible.

Remember that Christianity is all about a relationship. God wrote the Bible because he wants to know us. The more we read it, the more we know of God, the more we learn to admire and adore the God who so longs to be in relationship with us.

William Wilberforce, the man who gave his life to putting an end to the slave trade, used to say Psalm 119 to himself from memory when he was most under pressure.[1] This is quite impressive, because it's 176 verses long. Wilberforce chose that particular psalm because it's about the importance of relying on God's word.

> ➤ At this point, you might want to ask one of the leaders to give a testimony illustrating how the Bible has enabled them to know God.

However, did you notice the contrast in Psalm 1? There are those whose focus is on the Bible who are like strong, thriving trees, planted by fresh water. But, on the other hand, there are those who mock the Bible, and decide to live life their own way. What are they like? Look again at verse 4: "They are like chaff that the wind blows away." It's an image of a threshing floor after harvest, when great shovels lift the wheat and toss it into the air. The precious grain falls to the floor, but the chaff – the husks and the useless bits of straw – are scattered in the wind. And look at how the psalm continues in verses 5 and 6.

> ➤ Read aloud Psalm 1:5–6.

And that's what the wicked are said to be like: because they ignore the words of the One who made them, they have no future and they will perish.

That's the stark choice the psalm sets before us. Will we be like chaff, without roots, with no stability and no future? Or will we be like the tree, firmly grounded and nourished by what we read in the Bible?

Our destinies are determined by our choices.

In Luke chapter 10, there's a description of two sisters. Jesus has come to their house to visit, and the reactions of the two sisters are very different. Turn with me to Luke 10, and we'll read from verse 38.

> ➤ Read aloud Luke 10:38–42.

---

[1] Quoted in Charles Haddon Spurgeon, *Treasury of David*, Psalm 119, Introduction (Pasadena, TX: Pilgrim Publications, 1983). Spurgeon quotes William Alexander, *The Witness of the Psalms* (1877), which in turn quotes Wilberforce's diary.

CHRISTIANITY
EXPLORED

As Jesus teaches, Martha is occupied with preparing a meal for him. Mary – on the other hand – just sits down and listens. Martha seethes. She says, "Lord, don't you care...?"

Jesus very gently reminds her that she has a choice to make here. Whereas she has chosen to attend to details that keep her from hearing Jesus' teaching, her sister Mary has chosen to listen. And for Mary, that's the most important thing.

We always make time for the things that are most important to us. Martha wants to produce a meal for Jesus, *then* sit down and listen to him. There's nothing wrong with what Martha is doing. However, Jesus tells Martha that by making time to hear God's word, "Mary has chosen what is better."

The challenge for us in the midst of busy lives is the same: will we become caught up with social engagements, business responsibilities, travel plans and domestic chores – or will we choose to spend time listening to God's word?

Will we continue to live as the world lives, or will we choose what is better?

Let me leave you with the following questions for your groups:

➤ *Display the following questions and read them aloud.*

• **"Mary has chosen what is better" (Luke 10:42). What choices do you need to make to hear God's word?**

• **The person who delights in God's word is "like a tree planted by streams of water, which yields its fruit in season" (Psalm 1:3). Do you think the Bible could play this role in your life?**

➤ *Allow 30 minutes for groups to work together through the* Study Guide *section called GROUP DISCUSSION.*

➤ *It may be useful to have Bible reading notes available to help participants who want to begin reading the Bible for themselves. You (and any other leaders) might also want to share with participants how and when you do your own personal study of the Bible.*

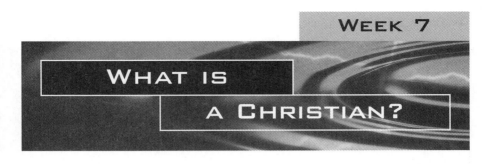

WHAT IS A CHRISTIAN?

➤ *Welcome the course participants and suggest they take 20 minutes to work through the* Study Guide *section called GROUP DISCUSSION 1 with their group.*

➤ *Deliver the talk. The wording below is intended only as a general guide. The aim of the talk is to recap what the course has covered so far about Jesus' identity and mission, and then to explain what Jesus demands of those who want to follow him.*

A little boy at Sunday school is asked to draw a picture of Mary, Joseph and the baby Jesus on their flight into Egypt. The teacher had been telling them about the time in Matthew chapter 2 when an angel appears to Joseph in a dream and warns him to flee with his family from the murderous King Herod. So the little boy carefully draws a picture of a huge airplane and, when the teacher asks him what it is, he points out that it's "the flight into Egypt," indicating Joseph, Mary and the baby Jesus who are sitting happily in the passenger seats. "But who's that?" asks the teacher, indicating a shadowy figure in the cockpit. Growing a bit tired of all the stupid questions, the little boy says, "That's Pontius Pilot."

It's not only five-year-olds who misunderstand what Christianity's about. There must be millions of people in this country alone who have rejected what they *think* is Christianity, but who have actually rejected something that is only a pale imitation of the real thing. There must also be a great many Christians who have lost sight of the basics. I want to look now at Mark chapter 8 in order to find out exactly what it means to be a Christian. In this chapter, we see Jesus explaining that a Christian is someone who knows who Jesus is, understands why he came, and is prepared to follow him – whatever the cost.

➤ *Display the following headings.*

Who is Jesus?

Why did Jesus come?

What does Jesus demand?

WHO IS JESUS?

So question 1: who is Jesus? This question has dominated the book of Mark up to chapter 8, and we, the readers, already know the answer. As we've seen, Mark has told us the answer in the very first verse, where he writes that this is a book about Jesus Christ, "the Son of God."

You might think that would drain the book of all interest, but the fact is that *the disciples don't know what we know.* And so we follow them around, watching as they try to make sense of Jesus. Jesus, for his part, forces them to ask questions about who he is by doing amazing things – as we've seen. They watch him calming a violent storm, curing incurable illness, bringing a little girl back from the dead. They even hear him claiming to be able to forgive sin. And yet they don't come up with the obvious answer: that this is God's Anointed One, the Christ, the Son of God, the one who'd been promised throughout the Old Testament. They were expecting it, were desperately hoping for it, but now that he's there, standing right in front of them, they just don't see it.

Have you ever seen one of those "trick" pictures that seem to show one thing but – looked at another way – show something entirely different? The most well-known one is probably the picture of a beautiful young woman that can also look like a hideous old hag.

➤ *Display the picture on the next page. (It can also be downloaded from the website at www.christianityexplored.com)*

CHRISTIANITY
EXPLORED

I have to admit that despite staring at that picture for a long time, it was ages before I could see the beautiful young woman. All I saw was the hideous old hag. And if you're an amateur psychologist, I'm sure you could have some fun with that fact.

Well, in a similar way, Jesus also had two faces: the human and the divine. The two were obvious, they were there for all to see, but even though the disciples stared and stared for several years, all they could see was the man. They couldn't see the divine face of Christ. Mark draws our attention to their blindness again and again. For example, he does it in chapter 8, verses 17 and 18. Jesus is exasperated with the disciples: "Do you still not see or understand? Are your hearts hardened? Do you have eyes but fail to see, and ears but fail to hear?" And then, quite strikingly, the next incident we read about is Jesus enabling a blind man to see. Look at Mark 8, verses 22 to 26.

➤ *Read aloud Mark 8:22–26.*

The miracle is unique. It's the only one of Jesus' miracles that happens *gradually*. First, Jesus touches the blind man, and he begins to see, but only vaguely. Then, he touches him again, and this time the man sees perfectly. Mark wants us to see this as a parallel to the gradual opening of the *disciples'* eyes. Of course, the disciples aren't *physically* blind; they are *spiritually* blind. But – either way – they still need Jesus to heal them.

Then, in verses 27 to 29, we see their spiritual blindness begin to be cured. They won't be fully cured until later, when they understand what Jesus came to do and what it means to follow him, but here, for the first time, is an indication that they know *who Jesus is.*

➤ *Read aloud Mark 8:27–29.*

This is a big step forward for the disciples. Finally, they've recognized that Jesus is the Christ, the King promised in the Old Testament, who would have the power and authority of God himself. Jesus asks them a scorching question here: "Who do you say I am?" It's very personal. And at this point in Mark's Gospel, it also gets very personal for *us*. Who do *we* say Jesus is? What do *we* see as we look at the face of Jesus? Do we just see the human face or can we see the divine face as well?

But it's not enough simply to know Jesus' true identity. Peter gets the question of Jesus' identity absolutely right here, but when it comes to the question of what Jesus came to do, Peter gets it horribly wrong.

WHY DID JESUS COME?

And so we move on to answer the second question – why did Jesus come? Look at the next verse – verse 30.

➤ *Read aloud Mark 8:30.*

Now that the disciples have seen who he is, what is Jesus' response? He warns them not to tell anyone about him. You see, at this point, their eyes are only half open. Jesus knows that although they can see who he is, they don't yet see why he's come or what it means to follow him. And that's why he tells them not to tell anyone about him yet.

Then Jesus begins to teach them more about himself. It's as if he's starting to correct their partial vision. Look at verses 31–32.

➤ *Read aloud Mark 8:31–32.*

That's why Jesus came. He came to die. In fact, it's necessary that he die. And Jesus knows that very well. He knows that the only way in which sinful people can be brought back into a relationship with God is if he dies in our place.

CHRISTIANITY
E✝PLORED

But Peter has this image of Jesus as king so clearly in his mind that it seems entirely inappropriate to him that Jesus would have to die. And he tells Jesus so. He takes him aside and gives him a pep talk. How on earth can a king bring in his kingdom by *dying*? That's ridiculous. But Jesus tells Peter that he's got it all wrong. Look at verse 33.

➤ *Read aloud Mark 8:33.*

In a way, I don't blame Peter for thinking like this. After all, there are two ways of looking at the cross. If, as Jesus says, we have in mind "the things of men," there is tremendous weakness at the cross. Jesus seems exposed, humiliated, and defeated. From the human point of view, the cross seems to prove conclusively that Jesus has got it all wrong. He was right about so many things, but if he really *was* the Son of God, why couldn't he come down from the cross? A king should be on a throne, not a cross.

But what do we see if we look at the cross from another angle – from God's perspective? What if we have in our minds, as Jesus says, "the things of God"? Then we can see the cross as part of God's rescue plan. We can see that Jesus *chooses* to be separated from God so that we don't have to be, paying the terrible price for our sin, being executed – in our place – for crimes he never committed. From God's perspective, and from ours if we have in mind the things of God, this is not weakness. In fact, there has never been a more powerful moment in history.

On 13 January 1982, millions of television viewers watched as a balding, middle-aged man swam in the icy cold water of a river in Washington DC.[1] Seven inches of snow had fallen that day. The water was so cold that life expectancy was no more than a few minutes. A helicopter quickly reached the scene, and let down a rope to haul the man to safety. The viewers at home were amazed as the man twice grabbed hold of the rope, *then quite deliberately let it go*. Each time the rope was lowered to him, he had a chance of survival, but he chose to let it go. And – in front of millions of avidly watching viewers – the man eventually died.

It seems like a futile and pointless death. But we need to see the broader picture.

Five minutes earlier, a Boeing 737 jetliner carrying eighty-three passengers and crew had departed from National Airport's main runway. However, the ice that had built up on the wings as it waited for take-off prevented it from gaining sufficient

---

[1] See *Wrath of God: Death in the Potomac: The Crash of Flight 90* (produced by the History Channel, 2000).

altitude, it hit a bridge heavy with commuters and then plunged nose-first into the frozen Potomac River. The survivors struggled in the freezing river amid ice chunks, debris, luggage, seat cushions and jet fuel. Thankfully, a rescue helicopter arrived and let down its rope. The television cameras then pick out a balding, middle-aged man. He grabs the rope, and *deliberately* gives it to somebody else, who is then pulled to safety. The man does this twice before – exhausted – he drowns. When we have all the details in front of us, an apparently futile death is shown to be purposeful, daring and amazingly loving.

And Jesus' death is all of those things. He also died as part of a rescue mission. In his amazing love he came to earth and died in our place, taking the punishment that we deserved, so that we could enter into a relationship with God. He was forsaken so that we need never be. There are two ways of seeing the cross. We can see it from a human perspective, as a pathetic and needless death. Or we can see it from God's perspective, as our only means of rescue. Our lives, as well as our deaths, will be determined by the way in which we respond to what Jesus did on the cross.

WHAT DOES JESUS DEMAND?

And that leads us to our third question: what does Jesus demand? It is not enough to recognize who Jesus is, or even why he came. Just like the disciples, we also need to understand what it means to follow him. Look at Mark 8, verse 34.

➤ *Read aloud Mark 8:34.*

According to Jesus' words here, following him requires a change of allegiance. It also means responding to Jesus' call to die. Then, because these things are not easy, he goes on to give us a convincing reason for following him.

➤ *Display the following headings.*

A change of allegiance

A call to die

A convincing reason

CHRISTIANITY
E✝PLORED

A CHANGE OF ALLEGIANCE

First of all, Jesus demands a change of allegiance. "If anyone would come after me, he must deny himself..." Denying self means no longer living for ourselves. And if you're not sure that you *do* live for yourself, try answering this question: who has the right to tell you how to live your life? Surely our instinctive response is to cry, "No one! No one has the right to tell me how to live, apart from me. *I'm* the only one who should decide what I do." But *God* made us, *he* sustains us, we are dependent on *him* for everything we have, and it is absurd to live in *God's* world as if *we* are the ultimate authorities over our lives.

So Jesus tells us to deny ourselves. He puts it another way in Mark chapter 1, when he tells us to "repent and believe the good news." The word "repent" literally means "to change one's direction." To "repent and believe" means I stop going my own way and instead say, "Lord Jesus, I recognize who you are, and from now on I will allow you to take charge."

"If anyone would come after me, he must deny himself..." It's a simple and brief instruction, just half a verse, but I want us to see that it is profoundly radical. There are real issues to grapple with: my time and how I use it; my money and what I do with it; my work and how I approach it; my sexuality and how I view it; my family and how I relate to them.

But Jesus' call is more than self-denial. You may have noticed that there's an additional ingredient to Jesus' command: "If anyone would come after me, he must deny himself *and take up his cross* and follow me." Not only must we deny ourselves if we are to follow him, we must also *take up our cross*.

A CALL TO DIE

Remember where Jesus himself is going at this point. He is heading for the cross, as he's just told the disciples. It is striking, and not a little disturbing, to see Jesus immediately turn his attention from the cross *he* must take up, to the cross *we* must take up. Jesus warns potential followers that if they are to follow him, they too must head for the cross. Although it's unlikely that any of us will face a literal cross, the command is still a chilling one. Jesus is telling us here that if we commit ourselves to him, it will mean a martyrdom of one kind or another. So this is Jesus' offer to his hearers: "I will die for you, but you must be prepared to die for me, if you want to follow me." It's a call to come and die.

In the early years of the twentieth century, the explorer Ernest Shackleton put an advertisement in various London newspapers to try and find men who would come with him on his polar expedition. The advertisement ran like this: "Men wanted for a hazardous journey. Small wages, bitter cold, long months in complete darkness, constant danger, safe return doubtful."[2] Needless to say, there weren't many applicants. But Christ's appeal is similar. Come and die.

Of course, Jesus isn't saying that everyone who follows him will face a violent death. But, at the very least, they will face suffering. His followers can find themselves marginalized, misunderstood and isolated. Why? Because friends, family, colleagues, and those around you may find your beliefs and conduct uncomfortable or even offensive. For example, if you stand up for Christ's claim to be "the way, the truth and the life,"[3] insisting that no-one can know God except through him, then you will face opposition.

A Christian is not only someone who sees clearly who Jesus is and why he came. A Christian is someone who is prepared to follow him, whatever the cost.

So with Jesus' call for a change of allegiance, comes a call to die. If you've grasped what that means, you will want to think very seriously before committing your life to Christ. There seems an awful lot to lose. With that in mind, Jesus goes on to give us a convincing reason for switching our allegiance to him.

A CONVINCING REASON

If we think about following Christ in purely earthly terms, the cost seems too high. So Jesus' aim in verses 35 to 37 is to give us the right perspective. Look at those verses with me.

➤ *Read aloud Mark 8:35–37.*

This passage insists that our "souls" are the most precious thing we have. If we lose our soul, there is *nothing* we can do to get it back.

By nature we tend to focus on our present circumstances. If something won't pay dividends *now*, people aren't very interested. But here Jesus wants to lift our eyes

---

[2] Julian Watkins, *The 100 Greatest Advertisements: Who Wrote Them and What They Did* (New York: Dover Publications, 1959).
[3] John 14:6

CHRISTIANITY
EXPLORED

from the present and fix them on the future. And the Bible says that the future is vitally important because it's eternal. When we die, it's not the end. Jesus teaches us here that there is a connection between how we live now and what will happen after death.

And there's a twist, because those who try to save their lives will lose them, while those who lose their lives will gain them. Jesus well knows how much we want to cling on to our lives, to do what we want to do when we want to do it. But he warns us that if we live in that way, then ultimately we'll lose the very thing we are so desperate to cling on to. He tells us that if we really want to hold on to our lives, there's only one option open to us: we must allow him to take control.

Christ will judge the world, whether we like it or not. And we can choose whether or not this judge will also be our rescuer. And ultimately, we will be treated very fairly. We will be treated by Jesus in exactly the same way as we have treated him, as he tells us in Mark chapter 8, verse 38.

➤ Read aloud Mark 8:38.

Because Jesus is the person who will return to judge the world, it is not a suicidal gesture to entrust him with my life. In doing so I know that my life will be saved. Moreover, whatever we might lose by following Christ pales into insignificance when we consider what awaits us in heaven. Jesus pleads with us to give up the very things that will destroy us – self-love, self-worship, self-will – and he pleads with us not to waste our souls.

In 1000 AD, 186 years after the death of Emperor Charlemagne, officials of the Emperor Otto re-opened Charlemagne's tomb.[4] Before them was an extraordinary sight. In the midst of all the finery buried with him – the gold, the jewels, the priceless treasure – there was the skeleton of Charlemagne himself, still seated on his throne, still wearing his crown. In his lap, there lay a Bible, and a bony finger rested on Mark chapter 8, verse 36: "What good is it for a man to gain the whole world, yet forfeit his soul?" I wonder what answer Charlemagne gave.

---

[4] Charlemagne – King of the Franks (768–814), King of the Lombards (774–814) and Emperor (800–814); b. 2 April c. 742, d. 28 January 814. His tomb in Aix au Chapelle was opened by Otto III (b. July 980, d. 23 January 1002) in AD 1000

Let me leave you with the following questions for your groups:

➤ *Display the following questions and read them aloud.*

• **"What good is it for a man to gain the whole world, yet forfeit his soul?" (Mark 8:36). How would *you* answer that question?**

• **Jesus said: "If anyone would come after me, he must deny himself and take up his cross and follow me" (Mark 8:34). Do you feel you could do this?**

• **"A Christian is someone who is prepared to follow Christ, whatever the cost." What is the cost?**

➤ *Allow 30 minutes for groups to work together through the* Study Guide *section called GROUP DISCUSSION 2.*

Before next week, it would be a great help if you'd do the HOME STUDY section in your *Study Guide*.

As we close our session, I want to say a few words about how we apply what we've learned from Mark. Please turn to Mark chapter 1, verse 15 and see what Jesus says there. "'The time has come,' he said. 'The kingdom of God is near. Repent and believe the good news!'" I don't know where you are with God or what you make of Jesus, but as you see here, the appropriate response to Jesus is to repent and believe. That means we turn from what we know is wrong and trust in what he has done for us on the cross.

Perhaps you are already a Christian. You've responded to what Jesus did on the cross by asking him to forgive you. You want to live a life that pleases him, in gratitude for all that he's done for you. Please keep coming, because the next three weeks will help you go on living for Christ.

Or perhaps you wouldn't call yourself a Christian, and you've still got questions, but you want to know more. I hope you'll find the next few weeks helpful in answering those questions – and let me say how grateful we are that you keep giving your time to understanding this.

Finally, perhaps you know that you are not a Christian, but you've been persuaded by what you've heard. You believe that Jesus is who he claims to be. You can see your own rebellion against God, your own need for rescue, and you want to accept God's forgiveness. Well, if that's you, then I want to give you a prayer that you can pray if you are ready to repent and believe. You are not under any pressure to do this but, if you are ready, this prayer gives you an opportunity to start the Christian life.

If you don't wish to pray this prayer now, then do bear with us. There is a copy of the prayer in your *Study Guide*, so you can take it home and think it through in private, if you'd prefer.

I'll read the prayer aloud once, so that you know exactly what it says, and then I'll pray it, inviting you to echo it in your heart if you want to.

> **Heavenly Father, I have rebelled against you. I have sinned in my thoughts, my words and my actions – sometimes unconsciously, sometimes deliberately. I am sorry for the way I have lived and ask you to forgive me. Thank you that Jesus died on the cross so that I could be forgiven. Thank you that I can now see clearly who Jesus is and why he came. Please send your Holy Spirit to help me follow him whatever the cost. Amen.**

➤ *Read the prayer again. Read slowly, giving participants time to echo it silently for themselves.*

And can I ask that if you did pray that prayer, do let one of your leaders know so that they can help you as you start the Christian life.

➤ *Thank everyone for coming and bring the evening to a close.*

CHRISTIANITY
E✝PLORED

CONTINUING
AS A CHRISTIAN

BEFORE THE TALK

➤ *Welcome the course participants and suggest they take 20 minutes to work through the* Study Guide *section called GROUP DISCUSSION 1 with their group.*

THE TALK

➤ *Deliver the talk. The wording below is intended only as a general guide. The aim of the talk is to warn that Christians will face opposition from the world around them, from their own sinful nature, and also from the devil. The talk explains how to continue as a Christian despite this opposition.*

The movie *Saving Private Ryan*,[1] set during World War II, tells the story of a group of men who are given orders to rescue one single man from behind enemy lines in Normandy. We are told that his three brothers have all recently been killed in action, leaving him as the only child of a single mother. When the US Army Chief of Staff hears about the situation, he gives orders to protect this precious remaining son, Private James Ryan, and he sends out a team of soldiers to bring him back alive.

The rescue mission is extremely perilous, and one by one it claims the soldiers' lives. At one point their captain says, "This Ryan better be worth it. He'd better go home, cure some disease or invent the longer-lasting light bulb."

But the orders to rescue Ryan are obeyed, and in the final battle scene, set on a heavily-shelled bridge, as the Captain himself dies, he whispers his last words to a dumbstruck Private Ryan: "James – earn this – earn it."

---

[1] *Saving Private Ryan* (dir. Steven Spielberg; prod. Ian Bryce, Mark Gordon and Gary Levinsohn; Dreamworks SKG / Paramount Pictures, 1998).

Fifty years pass and, in the closing shots of the movie, we see an elderly James Ryan returning to Normandy with his wife, children and grandchildren. He kneels beside the grave of the captain and, as tears fill his eyes, he says, "My family is with me today. Every day I think about what you said to me that day on the bridge. I've tried to live my life the best I could. I hope that was enough. I hope that at least in your eyes I've earned what all of you have done for me." Then he turns to his wife and asks with some anxiety, "Tell me I've led a good life. Tell me I'm a good man..."

In a way, the last words of the captain – "Earn it" – have crippled Ryan. Could he ever live up to the deaths of those young men? Private Ryan has lived his entire life with the last words of his rescuer ringing in his ears.

But Jesus' last words – recorded in John's Gospel chapter 19, verse 30 – are very different. As he dies to rescue us, Jesus doesn't say "Earn it." He says: "It is finished." They, too, are words that have the power to affect the course of a life.

As Jesus died on the cross to rescue you and me from sin, judgement and hell, he uttered those staggering words: "It is finished." The word in the Greek is actually a single word, "*tetelesti.*" It is in the past tense and it means "it is complete." This is the word a builder might shout when he places the final slate on the roof of a house he has built. Or the word a couple might use when they finally pay off their twenty-five year mortgage. *Tetelesti* – it is finished.

And notice that it's not "I am finished," as if this was a last desperate, self-pitying cry of surrender, a concession of defeat or failure. No, it's an exclamation of completion, of achievement, of triumph – "It is finished."

So, as he dies to rescue me, Jesus doesn't say, "Earn this [Rico], earn it." No, he says, "[Rico], it is finished. Your sin – past, present and future – is all forgiven." It is finished. I can't earn it, I can't pay for it, I've done nothing to deserve it. But Christ died for me to pay for my sin, to bring me back into a relationship with my loving Creator.

But this wonderful relationship won't be plain sailing. Christians will face opposition: from the world around them, from their own sinful nature, and also from the devil, who wants to undermine the Christian's relationship with God.

So firstly, there will be opposition from the world. If you stand up for Christ's words, if you remind people that they are living in God's world, that they're accountable to him, there will be times when you will be frozen out by people – even by those you love. It can be a painful experience to find yourself politely ignored or even verbally attacked by those closest to you. Jesus himself found that those who thought they knew him best – those he'd grown up with – resented the claims he made, and were offended by him. So if people are offended by us, it's a great comfort to know that things were no different for Jesus. In John 15, verses 18 onwards, Jesus warns us very clearly about this: "If the world hates you, keep in mind that it hated me first... If they persecuted me, they will persecute you also."

Second, all Christians will face opposition from their own sinful nature. As Paul says in Romans 7, verses 18 and 19: "I know that nothing good lives in me, that is, in my sinful nature. For I have the desire to do what is good, but I cannot carry it out. For what I do is not the good I want to do; no, the evil I do not want to do – this I keep on doing." And if that is true for Paul, who was one of the most godly Christians who ever lived, then it will certainly be true for us.

And third, there's opposition from the devil. What do you think about the devil? For lots of people, he's a joke figure: the man in the red tights with the unconvincing horns and the plastic pitchfork. He's not a threat; he's a joke.

The passage we read earlier in our GROUP DISCUSSION mentioned him, and this may be a shock to you, but the Bible insists that there *are* evil powers at work who will try to make you doubt the truth, who will lie to you and tempt you. The Bible explains that there are powerful and intelligent forces that are out to undermine the Christian and anyone who is even thinking of becoming one.

Jesus teaches that the devil's opposition is serious: even when people are listening to God's word being taught, he is at work. The last thing he wants is for people to put their trust in Christ and be saved. Jesus points this out in Luke chapter 8, verse 12, making it plain that people can hear God's words but then find that: "the devil comes and takes away the word from their hearts, so that they may not believe and be saved."

Christians are involved in an unseen spiritual battle. Please turn with me to Ephesians chapter 6, and we'll read verses 10–12.

➤ *Read aloud Ephesians 6:10–12.*

How does the devil fight? He schemes. He fights subtly, with no moral principles, no code of ethics.

Jesus calls him the "father of lies."[2] He's always trying to put lies into people's heads – things like, "Look, God's invisible. He's invisible because he's not there! This isn't the real world. This isn't reality. Forget about it."

Another name for the devil in the Bible is "the accuser."[3] And it's a very appropriate title, because he's always pointing to your failures. "If you were a real Christian, you would stop sinning. How can you call yourself a Christian when you keep doing this or that?" Or, "Remember that terrible thing you did. There's no way you can become a Christian."

And when you hear things like that, it's absolutely vital to remember those last words of Jesus: "It is finished." That's why Jesus came – *because* we're sinners. Once you've put your trust in Christ, it's finished.

Now, having said all that, let me say that to blame the devil for every single mishap, inconvenience or unpleasantness is unwise. It is dangerous to underestimate the devil's power, but it can be equally damaging to overestimate it. The Bible says that – thanks to the cross – the devil has already been defeated. As Revelation chapter 12 explains, "he knows that his time is short."

In the face of opposition from the world, from the sinful nature and from the devil, there are three great assurances that help Christians.

➤ *Display the following headings and read them aloud.*

The witness of the Spirit

The word of the Father

The cross of Christ

THE WITNESS OF THE SPIRIT

As we saw on the weekend / day away, the Holy Spirit gives believers the strength and the desire to battle against their sinful nature. In fact, this feeling of inner conflict – between the Spirit and the sinful nature – is strangely comforting, because it confirms that the Spirit is real and at work.

---

[2] John 8:44.
[3] Revelation 12:10

CHRISTIANITY
E✝PLORED

The Spirit also assures the Christian that he or she is indeed one of "God's children," no longer separated from him, and destined to be with him in heaven. For Christians in the midst of opposition, that assurance of eternal life is a very precious thing indeed.

THE WORD OF THE FATHER

Christians can also be sure of their relationship with God because of his promises to them in the Bible.

C. S. Lewis's book *The Screwtape Letters*[4] contains imaginary letters written by a senior devil to a junior devil. The senior devil wants to teach the junior devil how to cause a man who has become a Christian to waver in his faith. And the first tactic he recommends is to make the man rely totally on his feelings. Now, don't get me wrong, our emotions are God-given – they're part of what it is to be human. But if they're all we have to go on, then we will start to doubt our faith.

No matter what we feel – and as all of us know, our feelings can change with the weather – there are certain things we can be sure of. In times of anxiety, indecision, loneliness or temptation, we must remind ourselves of those certainties by reading and trusting the words of the infinitely powerful, infinitely loving God.

Let me read you two of God's promises in the Bible:

➤ *Read aloud Hebrews 13:5 (from "God has said…") and John 5:24.*

Reality is not determined by what we feel. It is determined by God's promises, which tell me that I am a Christian, that I am forgiven and that I am going to heaven because of what Christ has done. God has given me his word about these things.

Time and again, when clergy visit people who are dying, they find that people often feel very guilty about a particular thing they've done in their lives. You can ask the person, "Are you sorry? Have you asked God's forgiveness? Have you asked the wronged person's forgiveness?" And they will often answer "yes" to all three questions. But they still feel desperately guilty.

It's at moments like these – when guilty feelings persist – that Christians need to trust the word of God. Look at 1 John chapter 1, verses 8–9:

---

[4] C. S. Lewis, *The Screwtape Letters* (London: Fount, 1998).

> *Read aloud 1 John 1:8–9.*

So if you're feeling guilty about something, even though you've already asked God for forgiveness, let me ask you this: "Do you think your sin is covered by the words 'all unrighteousness'?" If so, do you trust God's promise here? God is promising that he will forgive all your sins – past, present and future. No matter what you've done, you are forgiven. You don't have to feel guilty anymore.

THE CROSS OF CHRIST

The third assurance of a Christian's relationship with God is the cross of Christ. As we've seen, Jesus doesn't tell us to "Earn it." He died on the cross saying, "It is finished." You're in a relationship with God not because you deserve it, not because you've earned it or because you've done enough or been good enough, but because you've trusted in what Christ has already done for you. You're at peace with God and you're going to heaven.

As the apostle Paul says at the beginning of Romans chapter 8: "there is now no condemnation for those who are in Christ Jesus."

AT THE END OF THE TALK

Let me leave you with the following questions for your groups:

> *Display the following questions and read them aloud.*

- **Do you feel able to trust God's promises in the Bible?**

- **Can you see how Jesus' words – "It is finished" (John 19:30) – might affect your life?**

> *Allow 30 minutes for groups to work together through the* Study Guide *section called GROUP DISCUSSION 2.*

AT THE END OF THE DISCUSSION

Before next week, it would be a great help if you'd do the HOME STUDY section in your *Study Guide*.

CHRISTIANITY
E✝PLORED

CHOICES
- KING HEROD

BEFORE THE TALK

➤ *Welcome the course participants and suggest they take 20 minutes to work through the Study Guide section called GROUP DISCUSSION 1 with their group.*

THE TALK

➤ *Deliver the talk. The wording below is intended only as a general guide. The aim of the talk is to help participants continue to wrestle with what it means to repent and believe, as we examine Herod's refusal to do so.*

I'm sure you've all seen magazines like this.

➤ *Hold up a copy of "Men's Health" magazine or similar.*

Every edition has articles about losing weight, keeping fit and eating healthily. Now obviously, in order to see any results, you have to choose to do what they say. And that's the difficult part. So often we choose not to do what we know is good for us. But unfortunately, as someone once said, "We are the choices we have made." And some of us only have to look down at our stomachs to see the truth of that statement.

Please turn to Mark chapter 6. We're going to look at verses 17–28. Because it's here that we read the story of Herod, a man who really does pay the price for the choices he makes.

➤ *Read aloud Mark 6:17–28.*

This grisly passage has fired the imaginations of artists and composers over the centuries. It brilliantly illustrates the fact that "we are the choices that we have made." In this passage Herod made two key choices: he chose to rebel and he chose not to repent.

➤ *Display the following headings.*

Herod chose to rebel

Herod chose not to repent

HEROD CHOSE TO REBEL

This isn't Herod the Great, the man who murdered all the baby boys living in the Bethlehem region when Jesus was born. This is his son, Herod Antipas, who is the ruler of Galilee.

Note that Herodias is not Herod's first wife. Herod's first marriage had lasted over twenty years. But then, while visiting his brother Philip, he met Philip's wife, Herodias. He allowed himself to fall in love with her and he proposed marriage. Herodias accepted, but only on the condition that he got rid of his present wife. Herod agreed.

So she left her husband, Herod's own brother, and came to live with Herod in Galilee. By doing this, Herod is choosing quite deliberately to rebel against God's law. Does he *know* he's rebelling? Yes, because this man John – who Herod knows is "a righteous and holy man" – has been bravely telling King Herod that "it is not lawful for you to have your brother's wife."

John, you may remember, is the man we met right at the beginning of Mark's Gospel. Also known as John the Baptist, this man told people about Jesus and urged them to turn away from their sin in order to be forgiven by God.

Herod puts John in prison, but he continues to listen to him: "When Herod heard John he was greatly puzzled; yet he liked to listen to him." Note that the word "puzzled" here doesn't mean that John's words were complicated. It means that Herod was disturbed by John's teaching.

CHRISTIANITY
E✝PLORED

Why? Because he had exposed Herod's rebellion. Perhaps as you've come on *Christianity Explored*, you have had a similar experience. Perhaps you've come to realize that you've been living your life for yourself, and ignoring the God who made you. Perhaps, like Herod listening to John, you listen to the words of Jesus and want to go on listening, despite the disturbance they cause.

So Herod continued to listen. Day after day it went on. The people at the palace must have thought that their king had gone religious, listening to this strange figure preach as he did. "Herod feared John" to the extent that he even "protected him," but there was nevertheless something that Herod was *not* prepared to do.

HEROD CHOSE NOT TO REPENT

Yes, he was prepared to listen to John. He was prepared to acknowledge John as a righteous and holy man. He was even prepared to protect John. But there was one thing he would not do. He would not cease his adultery. He would not repent.

Remember how we've seen that the right response to having our rebellion against God exposed is to repent. It is to do an about-turn, to turn from our sin and ask God for forgiveness.

But Herod wouldn't do that.

Then one day, on his birthday, Herod gives a banquet for his high officials and military commanders and the leading men of Galilee. Notice Mark's description of the banquet: "Finally the opportune time came." Herod's birthday is described as an opportunity. It's an opportunity for Herod to repent decisively and publicly, but it's also an opportunity for Herodias to get rid of John. Notice who seizes the opportunity, and who misses it.

During the birthday banquet, Salome, the daughter of Herodias, comes in and dances in front of all the men. The phrase "she pleased Herod and his dinner guests" has sexual overtones. As a result of her dance the king utters a ridiculous promise to this teenage girl. He says, in verse 23, "Whatever you ask I will give you, up to half my kingdom."

And I'm sure as he said it, all his friends were laughing and clapping him on the back. Salome runs to her mother Herodias – who extraordinarily has allowed her daughter to do this. "What shall I ask for? Diamonds, gold, rubies, or the lovely meadows to the south so we can establish great lands and farms?" "No, no," snaps her mother, "you ask for the head of John the Baptist." Herodias seizes her opportunity to get rid of John. We read, "At once the girl hurried in to the king with the request: 'I want you to give me right now the head of John the Baptist on a platter.'"

Well, that soon wipes the smile from Herod's face. We read that he was "greatly distressed." And, suddenly, we reach the key moment in Herod's life. He is suddenly in an extremely dangerous place. If "we are the choices we make," then this choice will have a profound effect on what Herod will become. And it's a terribly hard choice to make, considering all the oaths he's made, and all the guests he's trying to impress.

But there it is. Either he says, "Look, I shouldn't have made the oaths I made – it was a stupid thing to do. I can't kill John. He's a good man. I know the things he's said have been hard to accept, but he's always spoken the truth. I will not kill him." Or, alternatively, he can cave in to the fierce pressure of those around him, gamely pretending to laugh with all his guests, and suppressing his conscience one more time.

What will he choose?

Verse 26 says, "The king was greatly distressed, but because of his oaths and his dinner guests, he did not want to refuse her." Much as he feared John, he feared his guests more. Verse 27 continues, "So he immediately sent an executioner with orders to bring John's head. The man went, beheaded John in the prison, and brought back his head on a platter. He presented it to the girl, and she gave it to her mother."

It's horrific, isn't it? Tradition has it that she pulled the tongue out and pierced it with one of her pins: "That'll teach John to speak to me like that." You see, under pressure, this king has capitulated. He has allowed the head that warned him, the tongue that told him to turn from his rebellion and repent, to be literally cut off.

CHRISTIANITY
E⨍PLORED

But how many of us would have done something similar in Herod's position? The fact remains that many, many people will do just that: in the moment of decision, they will deny what they know is right because of what the family will think, what business colleagues may do, or because of what friends will say. Or because they know it will mean changing much-loved habits.

I wonder if you see the parallels Mark wants us to draw between John and Jesus?

Both preached the same message: that we need to turn from our rebellion against God and accept the rescue he has lovingly provided. Both were protected by powerful men: Herod and Pontius Pilate, both of whom tried to remain neutral but could not. And both John and Jesus suffered violent deaths as a result.

There is, of course, one further point of comparison. Why were both John and Jesus killed? Because in both cases people would not *repent* and would not do what was right.

In Mark chapters 1 to 3, we saw Jesus' awesome power and authority. In chapters 4 and 5, we saw the power of his teaching and of his word. Yet at the beginning of chapter 6, we see him rejected by his "home town." Their familiarity with Jesus bred contempt, they were offended by him, and they rejected him.

Jesus' response in subsequent chapters is to take his preaching elsewhere. He instructs his disciples to do likewise, saying that if people will not listen, they should move on. That's the pattern: the message will be rejected by some, who will themselves be rejected because of their response.

Interestingly, Herod is mentioned a final time in the Gospels, in Luke chapter 23. Luke records that Pontius Pilate sends Jesus to Herod when he learns that Jesus is from the area Herod controls. The meeting between Herod and Jesus is ominous, not because of what is said, but rather because of what is *not* said.

Please turn with me to Luke 23, verse 8.

➤ *Read aloud Luke 23:8–9.*

You see, there comes a time, after repeatedly refusing to repent, when there is no longer an opportunity to do so. It is easy to put it off, to say that we don't have the time, to think that we have too much to lose. *Surely it's better to wait*, you may well be thinking, *there'll be a more convenient time in the future*. Of course, it's *never* easy to repent. There will never be a "convenient" time. And Herod's story reminds us that we may not get an opportunity later.

When Herod gets no answer, he and his soldiers mock Jesus by dressing him in an elegant robe and sending him back to Pilate, who enjoys the joke. And look at verse 12. We read that on that day, "Herod and Pilate became friends – before this they had been enemies."

This should be a warning to us: rejecting Jesus' call to repent and believe may earn us the approval of other people, it may even win us friends, but it will eventually earn us the rejection of Jesus.

AT THE END OF THE TALK

Let me leave you with the following questions for your groups:

➤ *Display the following questions and read them aloud.*

- **Why do you think Herod refused to repent?**

- **John's preaching greatly disturbed Herod. How does Jesus' teaching make you feel?**

➤ *Allow 30 minutes for groups to work together through the* Study Guide *section called GROUP DISCUSSION 2.*

AT THE END OF THE DISCUSSION

Before next week, it would be a great help if you'd do the HOME STUDY section in your *Study Guide*.

CHRISTIANITY
E✟PLORED

CHOICES - JAMES, JOHN & BARTIMAEUS

➢ Welcome the course participants and suggest they take 20 minutes to work through the Study Guide section called GROUP DISCUSSION 1 with their group.

THE TALK

➢ Deliver the talk. The wording below is intended only as a general guide. The aim of the talk is to help participants wrestle with what it means to repent and believe. There is another opportunity to become a Christian after the talk and discussion.

"We are the choices that we have made." Last week we looked at the choices King Herod made. Tonight I'd like us to look at the choices made by some other people in Mark's Gospel. Let's turn to Mark chapter 10, and read verses 32–52.

➢ Read aloud Mark 10:32–52.

Did you see the choices people made in that passage? Let's look more closely at the choices James and John make, and the choice that Bartimaeus makes.

The context is there in verses 32–34. Jesus is leading the disciples and some others up to Jerusalem, and we read that they were astonished and frightened by Jesus' actions. Why? Remember that Jesus has already told them several times that the religious authorities will kill him. And these religious authorities are based in Jerusalem. So Jesus is marching deliberately into the jaws of death.

Look at the end of verse 33 – he says it again: he tells them that he will be condemned to death by the religious authorities and handed over to the Gentiles – in other words, the Roman authorities. They will mock him, spit on him, flog him and kill him. He will be condemned in the capital city Jerusalem by the nation's leaders.

Against that backdrop, two of his disciples – James and John – make a request that is breathtakingly inappropriate.

➤ *You will need to have the following headings ready for display, gradually revealing each of the headings as the talk progresses.*

The disciples' choice

Bartimaeus' choice

THE DISCIPLES' CHOICE

Look at verses 35–37.

➤ *Read aloud Mark 10:35–37.*

You see, although James and John have addressed Jesus as "teacher," it's obvious they haven't understood much of what he has taught, because they choose to ask Jesus for glory: "Let one of us sit at your right and the other at your left in your glory."

Now, as perverse as this seems after what Jesus has just said about dying, we shouldn't be surprised. It's not the first time the disciples have behaved like this. Towards the end of chapter 9, Jesus tells them that he will be betrayed and killed. And what's their response? Do they go into mourning, weeping that their beloved leader is going to be killed? No, they start arguing with each other about which one of them is the greatest!

Jesus' response then is the same as in the passage we've just read. He teaches them.

Jesus knows that James and John are missing the point when they ask to be seated on thrones either side of him. He takes them to task: "You don't know what you are asking." And he tries to correct their thinking. In verse 38 he says, "Can you drink the cup I drink or be baptised with the baptism I am baptised with?"

In the Old Testament, "the cup" generally referred to suffering. It also referred to the cup of God's wrath. The baptism language has the same meaning. So what Jesus is saying to James and John is: "Can you do what I will do? Can you bear the punishment that sin deserves? Can you bear God's judgement, and save others by

CHRISTIANITY
EXPLORED

doing so?" And the answer, of course, is that they can't. Like you and me, they need to be saved themselves from God's anger and judgement. As Jesus said, they don't know what they're asking.

Unfortunately, because James and John want glory, they don't see that Jesus' death is necessary. They anticipate that when Jesus' kingdom is established, there will be an unholy scramble for the best seats, so they judge it prudent to get in first by making an advance reservation. They want to be singled out. They are go-getters and status-seekers, they're very ambitious, hungry for fame and fortune. Suffering and death don't figure in their thinking.

And perhaps it's not surprising, when we remember the sort of background James and John had. We know that their father Zebedee had a household of servants because they are referred to in connection with their fishing business. And it may be that in following Jesus, James and John have missed having servants to wait on them. Maybe they were willing to leave their home and family and the fishing business and the servants, as long as they could be compensated with a little power and prestige.

And if we look at what's going on around us, I think we can see this lust for power almost everywhere. We see it in politics and in public life; we see it in big business and industry; we see it in the medical profession, the legal profession, in sports and in the arts. Sadly, we can also see it in the church. It's easy to turn the pulpit into a throne of authority and power.

When the other disciples hear about the request of James and John, we read that they became indignant. I wonder if they were indignant at the stupidity of James and John, or just annoyed that they hadn't got in there first?

But Jesus calls us along a different path. Look again at chapter 10 verse 42 and following:

➤ *Read aloud Mark 10:42–45.*

Those who are regarded as rulers in the pagan world boss people around, and their high officials exercise authority, but Jesus says: "not so with you." Four words I think we should underline in our Bibles: "not so with you."

James and John – like all of Christ's followers since – are not to embark on some kind of power trip, seeking prestige and status. Instead, they should follow the example their King sets. Look again at verse 45: "For even the Son of Man did not come to be served, but to serve, and to give his life as a ransom for many."

You see, Jesus uses his power *to serve*. That's the big contrast between James and John and Jesus. The last thing on the minds of James and John when they make their request of Jesus is *service*. They want nothing more than *to be served*, and what's worse, to be served by the very man who will save their lives.

By contrast, Jesus goes the way of the cross. He doesn't seek his own glory, but instead, in his concern for others, he walks deliberately towards pain and humiliation. He only wants to serve. As he heads deliberately toward Jerusalem, he chooses a cross, not a throne, a crown of thorns instead of a crown of gold. Jesus turns things upside down: "...whoever wants to become great among you must be your servant, and whoever wants to be first must be slave of all."

The disciples have yet to grasp the truth that Jesus knows very well as he heads toward Jerusalem: that the only way to be great in God's kingdom is to humble oneself. To serve rather than be served. And if that is true for Jesus – a man with God's authority and God's power – it will certainly be true for us.

So we've seen that the disciples chose to ask for glory. But the blind man Bartimaeus chooses to ask for something very different.

BARTIMAEUS' CHOICE

➤ *Read aloud Mark 10:46–52.*

Bartimaeus is different from the disciples in many ways. In verse 47, he recognizes that Jesus is the "Son of David" – in other words, that he is God's King in God's world. In verse 51, rather than addressing Jesus as "teacher" like the disciples, Bartimaeus uses a word that means "Master" in the original language. So Bartimaeus says, "Master, I want to see." Ironically, even though they're not physically blind, that's exactly the request James and John should have made, because they're the ones who can't see what it means to follow Jesus. Also notice that while the disciples wanted Jesus to do whatever they asked, Bartimaeus asks for mercy. In other words, he recognizes that he deserves nothing from Jesus. He cries, "have mercy on me!"

CHRISTIANITY
E✝PLORED

Do you see how different he is to James and John? Bartimaeus' cry is not for power and status, but for mercy. And even when people tell him to be quiet, he keeps on asking. This blind man has seen who Jesus really is and what it means to follow him. In contrast, the disciples are blind.

So Jesus welcomes him and calls him and asks him the same question that he asked the disciples: "What do you want me to do for you?" And notice that while the disciples are rebuked by Jesus, Bartimaeus is healed: "'Go,' said Jesus, 'your faith has healed you.'" And literally that phrase means, "Your faith has saved you."

So, whereas James and John ask for status and receive a sharp rebuke, with Jesus insisting, "You don't know what you are asking," Bartimaeus asks for mercy and is saved.

How, then, should *we* respond to Jesus?

If you are someone who has put your trust in him already for your forgiveness, then you may need to learn the lesson that James and John learned: following Jesus is about service, not status.

But if you are someone who has not yet put your trust in Jesus for your forgiveness, then you need to do as Bartimaeus did: recognize who Jesus is, cry out to him for mercy, and follow him.

Let me leave you with the following questions for your groups:

➤ *Display the following questions and read them aloud.*

• **Who do you identify with most: James and John or Bartimaeus?**

• **What choices will *you* make based on what you've learned during *Christianity Explored*?**

➤ *Allow 30 minutes for groups to work together through the Study Guide section called GROUP DISCUSSION 2.*

CHRISTIANITY
E✝PLORED

As we finish the course, what choices do *you* need to make as a result of what you've learned during **Christianity Explored**? Some of you may still have questions, but some of you may have understood who Jesus is, why he came, and what it means to follow him. If that's you, then here is a prayer you can pray to begin your life following Jesus. It's the same prayer I read out in Week 7, and remember that there is a copy of the prayer in your *Study Guide*, so you can take it home and think it through in private, if you'd prefer.

I'll read the prayer aloud once, so that you know exactly what I'll be praying. Then, if you decide it's a prayer *you* want to pray, you can echo the words silently to yourself when I read it a second time.

Here's the prayer:

> **Heavenly Father, I have rebelled against you. I have sinned in my thoughts, my words and my actions – sometimes unconsciously, sometimes deliberately. I am sorry for the way I have lived and ask you to forgive me. Thank you that Jesus died on the cross so that I could be forgiven. Thank you that I can now see clearly who Jesus is and why he came. Please send your Holy Spirit to help me follow him whatever the cost. Amen.**

➤ *Read the prayer again. Read slowly, giving participants time to echo it silently for themselves.*

If you did pray that prayer, do let one of your leaders know so that they can help you as you start the Christian life.

I want to thank all of you for making time to come, and for contributing so much to the group. It's been a privilege to meet you. Please use the FEEDBACK FORM to let us know how you found the last ten weeks.

➤ *As this is the end of the course, expand upon the choices now available to participants (for example, follow-up courses, discipleship courses, or future **Christianity Explored** courses). Having just read through one book of the Bible, you might want to suggest that they pick one of the remaining 65 and read through that!*

ACKNOWLEDGEMENTS

My heartfelt thanks go first of all to Richard Bewes and the staff of All Souls Church, Langham Place for their prayers, their patience and their unfailing partnership in the gospel.

Other churches and organizations have also graciously lent great wisdom and expertise: Holy Trinity Brompton, St. Helen's Bishopsgate, UCCF and Willow Creek Church in Chicago. In addition, I gratefully acknowledge the support of the Australian clergyman, Michael Bennett, who authored an earlier course run at All Souls Church called Christianity Explained.

The following people have repeatedly and generously dedicated their time and their talents to this project: Diane Bainbridge, Emma Carswell, Andrea Clarke, Paul Clarke, Chris Hobbs, Rosemary Jubraj, Grace McDowell, Mark O'Donoghue, Grant Owens, Sophie Peace, Cath Semple, Emma Sloan, Tara Smith, Fe-yen Swainsbury, Anita Thomas, Tim Thornborough of the Good Book Company, Paul Williams and Michael You. And I am particularly thankful for the creative gifts of Barry Cooper and Sam Shammas, who have meticulously reworked the course material for this second edition.

Lastly, to the two men who led me to Christ, Christopher Ash, and my brother, George: I am forever in your debt.

Rico Tice
All Souls Church, Langham Place
London
May 2003